MANAGING YOUR INFORMATION

How to design and create a textual database on your microcomputer

Applications in Information Management
and Technology Series
Edited by Ching-chih Chen

Carol Tenopir
and Gerald Lundeen

Neal-Schuman Publishers
New York   London

Published by Neal-Schuman Publishers, Inc.
23 Leonard Street
New York, NY 10013

Library of Congress Cataloging-in-Publication Data

Tenopir, Carol
  Managing your information.
  (Applications in information management and
technology series; 5)
  Bibliogrphy: p.
  Includes index.
  1. Data base management. 2. Text processing
(Computer science) I. Lundeen, Gerald W. II. Title.
III. Series: Applications in information management
and technology series ; no. 5)
QA76.9.D3T42 1988   005.74   87-34894
ISBN 1-55570-023-3

Contents

List of Figures

Preface

Managing Your Information has grown out of a series of workshops we have offered over the last seven years, classes we teach at the School of Library and Information Studies (University of Hawaii at Manoa), and articles we write.

The workshops were in response to the great interest among many members of the library and information community in creating inhouse databases. In 1981, together with Pamela Cibbarelli, we began offering workshops on software evaluation and selection for inhouse retrieval systems. These workshops discussed specific software packages for the mainframe, mini, and micro environments. The microcomputer environment was easy; there were only a few suitable software packages to choose from in those days. This is no longer the case. There are now many software packages to choose from and the microcomputer world now offers some of the most exciting potential for database applications. The microcomputer makes an inhouse database much more possible for even small applications, and the number of good software packages now available makes the chance of success good.

In 1987 we offered a workshop that focused on microcomputer-based bibliographic database design. We found there was a wealth of material to convey on this narrow subject, and many issues in the microcomputer environment are unique. Concerns of large mainframe systems are often not relevant in a microcomputer system.

Within the Masters of Library and Information Studies degree program at the University of Hawaii, we teach several classes that relate to the topic of database design. Carol's class in Database Design and Creation includes many of the steps discussed in this book and gives students an opportunity to construct a textual database. Jerry's Information Storage and Retrieval and Library Automation classes include the foundations for many of the topics covered in this book, which has naturally evolved from all of these courses.

Managing Your Information can be used as a textbook in classes in textual database design or by the librarians, researchers, and others who want to create an access tool for textual information. We have included necessary background information on microcomputer hardware, software, and indexing, but have tried to emphasize practical how-to-do-it advice. As you go through this book you will be introduced to all of the steps necessary to create a textual database using your microcomputer. This book will not teach you the ins and outs of specific software packages, nor answer all questions that may be unique to your situation. It will provide you with general guidelines and information on every step in the design process, which can then be adapted by you to your special situation. The process has now been followed successfully by many of our students and workshop participants.

Many people have been involved with this book since the beginning stages. Most important are the students and the workshop attendees who have given us the feedback, constructive criticism, and support needed to complete this project. Parts of several student projects are included with special thanks to Beth Cook and Lindy Naj. Ho Kwan (Rita) Lo created several of the figures and verified citations and appendix information. Her cheerful help was invaluable. Ho Kwan Lo and Doreen Grant did the index.

Our editor, Ching-chih Chen, is ultimately responsible for giving us the encouragement to translate our years of workshops, classes, and journal articles into a book. Thanks to her both for her ideas and her enthusiasm.

Finally, we want to acknowledge the help of Alma and Wayne Lundeen. They gently pushed us to finish and saw us through the difficult final stages of the project. They were always there to help.

Carol Tenopir
Jerry Lundeen
Honolulu, HI

1

Textual Databases

This book is an introductory guide for the librarian, other information professional, student, or individual who wants to design and create a textual database using a microcomputer. Such databases are referred to as *private files, in-house databases,* or *personal files.* No matter what they are called, such files or databases can be defined as collections of computer searchable textual information created by an organization or an individual for use within that organization or by that individual. An inhouse textual database may be a collection of bibliographic records describing a reprint collection gathered by a researcher, a compilation of citations to all of the literature on a certain topic, descriptions of all of the books held by a special library, the complete texts of legislation pertaining to a certain industry, or an annotated list of names and addresses of community agencies. They all contain mostly words rather than statistics or numbers.

DEFINITIONS

Librarians and the online information industry typically refer to such textual collections as *databases.* More accurately they should be called *files* because they are usually a single discrete collection of information. The term databases is more precisely used to refer to a system that includes several individual files used for different purposes. Different parts of individual files may be used at the same time in a database configuration. For example, a library user file might contain names, addresses, and borrower status of all potential library users. A book file might contain bibliographic and copy information about all books in the library. In a database environment, information from the user file might be linked to information from the book file when a book is borrowed. The types of inhouse files described in this book usually stand alone. Because the term database has been accepted by the information community as a synonym for a single file, it will be used more frequently in this book.

1

Librarians and other information professionals are familiar with searching commercially available databases on the large vendor systems such as DIALOG, BRS, LEXIS/NEXIS, and WILSONLINE. As of January 1987, there were over 3,300 of these publicly available online databases listed in the Cuadra/Elsevier *Directory of Online Databases*. (This is an increase from 2,500 databases in 1985 and only 400 in 1979.) You may be surprised to know that you will be able to design and create an inhouse database that will have many of the same characteristics and searching features that are available on the much larger commercial systems. This process will not be completely without stumbling blocks or frustration, but with careful planning the final results should be successful.

TYPES OF DATABASES

Textual databases can be classified into three main types. *Bibliographic databases* are the type of databases most familiar to librarians. Figure 1.1 shows sample records from an inhouse bibliographic database. Bibliographic records provide a surrogate of a document that includes a bibliographic citation and other information that describes the content of a document. Sometimes they have subject descriptors and abstracts. Surrogates describe and point to documents, but do not contain the complete texts of the documents themselves. Bibliographic databases are the most common type of inhouse databases because many researchers or organizations maintain reprint, document, or book collections and because they use a relatively small amount of computer storage space.

Full text databases, in contrast, provide the complete texts of items. Figure 1.2 shows a sample record from a hypothetical full text database. Journal articles, statutes, correspondence, and company reports are some materials that are commonly included in full text inhouse databases. The storage requirements and conversion costs for such databases are still often prohibitive, so full text databases are not often created using a microcomputer. Since most organizations now use word processing to generate inhouse documents, conversion costs may no longer be a significant factor for some types of full text inhouse databases.

The third category of textual databases is the *referral* or *directory database*. Figure 1.3 shows sample records from a hypothetical inhouse referral database. Referral databases typically provide such things as names, addresses, phone numbers, and information about

FIGURE 1.1   Sample Bibliographic Database Records

AN	84031234
TI	Identification and Evaluation of Software for Microcomputer-based Inhouse Databases.
AU	Tenopir, Carol
CS	University of Hawaii at Manoa
JN	Information Technology and Libraries
PY	March 1984
CI	Vol. 3, Pgs. 21–34.
LA	English
AB	Discusses methods and sources for locating software packages suitable for inhouse textual databases. Describes the procedures for evaluating such software.
SU	Information Storage And Retrieval; Computer Software; Bibliographic Databases; Database Design; Microcomputers.

AN	81045678
TI	Microcomputers in Personal Information Systems.
AU	Lundeen, Gerald
CS	University of Hawaii at Manoa
JN	Special Libraries
PY	April 1981
CI	Vol. 72, Pgs. 127–137.
LA	English
AB	Discusses the potential of microcomputers for managing personal information collections. Reviews basic hardware and software considerations.
SU	Computer Software; Microcomputers; Bibliographic Databases; Information Storage and Retrieval; Researchers.

organizations or individuals. For example, a referral database in a public library might provide information about community organizations that offer adult education courses.

HARDWARE

Manual files of bibliographic, full text, and referral information have been kept within organizations for years. For the last three decades, many information providers have realized the advantages of using computers for such files. These advantages include such things as streamlined maintenance, ease in updating, increased search

FIGURE 1.2   Sample Full Text Database Record

AN	87012345
TI	Online Education: Planning for the Future
AU	Tenopir, Carol
CS	University of Hawaii at Manoa
JN	Online
PY	January 1987
CI	Vol. 11, Number 1, pgs. 65–66.
SH	Education; Library and Information Science; Online Database Searching
TX1	In the last decade, schools of library and information science have recognized the important role they play in educating online intermediaries. A survey in 1982 found that at that time 76% of all schools accredited by the American Library Association included online searching in their curriculum. In 1987 that percent is certainly higher.
TX2	Most of these courses to date have concentrated on the

.   .
.   .
.   .
.   .

TX14	. . .prepare students for all aspects of the information industry.
FN	Stephen P. Harter and Carol H. Fenichel, "Online Searching in Library Education," Journal of Education for Librarianship 23 Summer 1982: 3–22.
CP	The author.

capabilities, and the ability to easily copy the database contents. The increasing power of the microcomputer with its decreasing cost make inhouse databases an increasingly attractive option for small textual collections.

Inhouse databases can be created using an inhouse micro-, mini-, or mainframe computer. Microcomputers are typically controlled by the department creating the database, while mini- or mainframe computers may be centrally located in an organization for shared use by all departments. This book will focus on the use of microcomputers.

Since their introduction in the 1970s and widespread use after IBM entered the marketplace in 1981, microcomputers have had a major impact on information handling. The increased storage capacity now available on microcomputers allows the creation of relatively sophisticated inhouse databases at an affordable price. There are

FIGURE 1.3   Sample Referral Database Records

AN	123456
CN	The XYZ Corporation
AD	123 Maple Street
CY	Los Angeles ST CA ZP 90024
PH	(213) 555-6767
BU	Manufacturer of contact lenses and other eye care products.
YR	Started 1899
SC	6794
SA	$1.5 million
OF	John Smith, CEO; Mary Smith, President; Joe Smith, Vice President
EM	45 employees at this location
SQ	5000 square feet

AN	338405
CN	Boldic Electric Company, Limited
AD	2323 Kumu Street
CY	Honolulu ST HI ZP 96822
PH	(808) 945-0100
BU	Manufacturer of chip coil for export.
YR	Started 1983
SC	3401
SA	$75 million
OF	Roger Charles, CEO; Mary Ling, President; Lydia McCall, Vice President; John Liu, Vice President
EM	400 employees at this location
SQ	10,000 square feet

now many software packages on the market that take advantage of these developments.

The microcomputer environment is not without problems, however. Although each individual unit is relatively inexpensive, most microcomputers and database software allow only one user at a time. This means you may encounter queues or contention between file maintenance and database use. If the microcomputer is being used for applications other than the database, priorities may restrict or inhibit access to your database system. Some possible solutions to these limitations are given in Chapter 2.

Chapter 2 discusses hardware, including microcomputers, multi-user options, and peripherals, in the context of database design. We assume no background with hardware, but the chapter does not attempt to be a comprehensive tutorial. It focuses only on those aspects of hardware that are important for database creation. If you have a basic knowledge of microcomputer hardware, you may wish to just scan Chapter 2.

RECORD STRUCTURE

As anyone who has worked with publicly available databases knows, textual databases are typically made up of *records*, which are in turn composed of *fields*. In a bibliographic database, for instance, each record contains the citation and other information that describes a single document. Each record typically contains fields for author, title, source, date, abstract, and subject descriptors. Two typical records for a bibliographic database are shown in Figure 1.1. These records each contain 10 fields: Accession Number (AN), Title (TI), Author (AU), Corporate Source (CS), Journal Name (JN), Publication Year (PY), Citation (CI), Language (LA), Abstract (AB), and Subject Descriptors (SU).

A full text database may contain the same basic fields as a bibliographic database with the addition of a field or fields for the full text. Figure 1.2 designates the 14 TX fields for the paragraphs in the text. It adds another field for footnotes (FN) and one for picture captions (CP).

Figure 1.3 shows how the field structure of a referral database can be quite different from a full text or bibliographic database. As the database creator, you will decide what constitutes a record and learn how to designate what fields will be included in each record. Chapter 6 discusses these procedures.

CHARACTERISTICS OF TEXTUAL DATABASES

Textual databases tend to have identifiable characteristics that set them apart from other databases in an organization (e.g., an inventory database or payroll database) and that affect the design of inhouse databases. These characteristics, discussed in detail in Chapter 3, include

- They are mostly composed of alphabetic characters rather than numbers, and even when numbers are included they are often treated as characters (e.g., dates).

- The databases are often large, consisting of many hundreds of records or thousands of records.
- Each record tends to have many fields (e.g., author, title, source, date, call number, abstract, subject descriptors, etc.).
- The fields tend to be variable length (one record may have a five character title, while another may have a 200 character title).
- Many of the fields are lengthy (e.g., titles, abstracts, full text).
- The same or similar fields are present in most records.
- Fields often contain repeating values (e.g., multiple authors, several descriptors), but whether they repeat and how often they repeat varies from record to record.
- Most applications require searchable access to all or most of the fields in the records.
- Search capabilities are important to users—they want to search on most fields and to be able to combine words in many ways and use fairly sophisticated search techniques.

SOFTWARE

Special information retrieval software has been developed for textual inhouse databases to provide the best search and retrieval capabilities for such information. Chapter 7 describes software options and features of some representative software packages. The best of these packages offer features that have been developed over the last two decades for commercial online database systems. These features, that have evolved into a de facto standard for textual database search and retrieval, include

- inverted file structure
- Boolean logic operators (AND, OR, NOT)
- comparison operators (greater than, less than, equal to)
- set building
- truncation
- word proximity
- free text searching
- the ability to specify which fields in a record will be searched and displayed

Chapter 3 explains these and other search features in more detail.

DATABASE PLANNING

Design and creation of an inhouse database requires careful planning and systematic evaluation of alternatives. Each step in the planning process is covered in the subsequent chapters of this book. Emphasis is placed on recognizing users' needs and on evaluation of existing software choices. This is not primarily a book on Data Base Management Systems (DBMS). DBMS programs are approached as just one category of computer programs that may be considered for textual inhouse databases. Similarly, computer programming is not emphasized in this book. Textual databases have complex software requirements, needing programming skills beyond what could be covered in a single text. There are many software packages on the market that are specifically designed for textual inhouse databases that should be considered before attempting custom programming. We assume you will be evaluating and selecting an existing software package.

The first step in the database design process is a feasibility study as described in Chapter 4. This feasibility study identifies the needs of potential users, articulates the requirements of the people who will be creating and maintaining the database, determines hardware and financial or human resource constraints within your organization that may affect software choice and database design.

After the feasibility study is complete, certain preliminary editorial decisions must be made. The initial editorial decisions (covered in Chapter 5) include defining the scope of the database contents; determining which fields (if any) should be created with authority lists; deciding whether controlled vocabulary subject descriptors should be added, and, if so, deciding whether a thesaurus should be constructed or whether an existing thesaurus could be used; and determining whether abstracts or summaries should be included. In connection with these decisions, database designers need to decide whether to include the full text of information or just a bibliographic record. Chapter 5 summarizes the factors that must be considered when deciding between bibliographic and full text information.

Once the initial editorial decisions are made, the actual database design begins with the record description, field structure definition, and field characteristics decisions. These decisions are incorporated into a *data dictionary*, an important preliminary step before software can be evaluated. The data dictionary may change somewhat after a specific software package is chosen. Chapter 6 explains how to do this preliminary definition.

Required or desired search features must next be defined and put into priority order in accordance with the needs analysis. Readers who are unfamiliar with the features offered by commercial database systems (such as DIALOG, BRS, or ORBIT) should read Chapter 3 before doing the needs analysis to familiarize themselves with the common search features of information retrieval systems. Chapter 3 also discusses the different ways that computer software deals with databases to make searching possible. It focuses on the file structures most likely to be encountered in database software and discusses the implications of each on search capabilities.

Chapters 7 and 8 cover the selection of software for inhouse databases. Evaluation and selection can only be done within the context of your specific situation as defined in your feasibility study, but there are certain identifiable options and choices within each option. Custom programming, adapting a general purpose DBMS, using a general purpose file management program, or purchasing special purpose software such as an information storage and retrieval package, library applications software, or a bibliography generator are all discussed in Chapter 7. Chapter 8 outlines the software evaluation process and includes two software evaluation forms.

The actual creation of the database begins when software and hardware are selected. Input options and ongoing procedures for such things as updating, maintenance, backup, and quality control are discussed in Chapter 9. Documentation, the step that at last brings the database to your inhouse users, is discussed in Chapter 10. Developments in hardware, software, and publishing that will have an impact on future inhouse database design are covered in the final chapter, Chapter 11. Appendixes include such information as a list of selected software packages, sources for identifying additional packages, suggested sources of software reviews, and a case study illustrating the development of an inhouse database for medical practitioners. Further readings are given in each chapter.

Your inhouse database is more likely to be a success if it meets the needs of the users, is carefully planned, and is well designed. The chapters of this book lay out a course of action to help ensure the successful design and creation of an inhouse textual database in any kind of organization.

FURTHER READING

Burton, Paul F., compiler. *Microcomputers in Library and Information Services: An Annotated Bibliography*. London: Gower, 1986.

Cuadra Associates. *Directory of Online Databases*. New York: Cuadra/Elsevier, 1982–. Quarterly.

Fidel, Raya. *Database Design for Information Retrieval: A Conceptual Approach*. New York, John Wiley & Sons, 1988.

Frankin, J. "Tools for Creating an In-House Database." *Proceedings of the 9th International Online Information Meeting*, 243–247. Medford, N.J.: Learned Information, 1985.

The Generation and Management of Small Scale Databases: Papers and Discussion. Canberra: Library Association of Australia, 1982.

Hlava, Marjorie. *Private File Creation, Database Construction*. New York: Special Libraries Association, 1984.

Lundeen, Gerald. "Microcomputers in Personal Information Systems." *Special Libraries* 72 (April 1981): 127–137.

Tenopir, Carol. "Data Base Design and Management." In *The Theory and Practice of Information Science*. Edited by John Olsgaard. Chicago: American Library Association, 1988. In press.

Williams, Martha E. "Electronic Databases." *Science* 228 (26 April 1985): 445–456.

Woods, Lawrence A. and Pope, Nolan F. *The Librarian's Guide to Microcomputer Technology and Applications*. Published for the American Society for Information Science. White Plains, N.Y.: Knowledge Industry Publications, Inc., 1983.

2

Hardware Options

A basic rule of computer system design is that one chooses the software first, then the hardware that is compatible with the software selected. In reality, this is not always followed. If you already have a microcomputer and do not want to consider the purchase of another, this may limit your options.

With a few notable exceptions, when designing microcomputer-based textual databases, the software available is written for PC DOS/MS DOS systems. There are enough exceptions, however, so that if possible the above rule should be followed. Exceptions on the high end of the microcomputer spectrum include STAR, which runs on Alpha Micro hardware with its AMOS operating system, and BRS Search for Micros, which runs on a number of UNIX based systems. On the low end of the spectrum there are some software packages running on CP/M micros or on the Apple II series.

A microcomputer system for database implementation requires several hardware components. This chapter examines the hardware components that may combine to make up such a system. We present a brief overview here—the reader is referred to the list of additional readings for more detail. The basic components are diagrammed in Figure 2.1.

CPU

The *central processing unit* (CPU) actually performs the data manipulation required by the software. In microcomputers the CPU is a microprocessor; all the essential circuitry is on a single silicon chip, which is built into a plug-in component approximately the size of a stick of chewing gum. The CPU is designed with an instruction set "hard wired" into the chip. This instruction set determines the machine language for the CPU. All programs that are run on a particular computer must be translated into the machine language for that computer.

11

FIGURE 2.1   Parts of a Computer

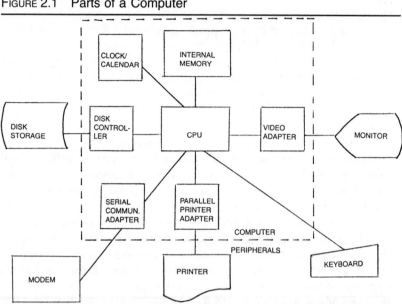

In the early years of microcomputers (1974–81) a fairly realistic rule of thumb for distinguishing microcomputers, minicomputers, and mainframes was based on the CPU word length. Microcomputers had a word length of eight bits, minis had a word length of 16 bits, and mainframes had 32 bits or more. The word length of a computer is the size of the unit of information it works with in its basic operations. Word size is determined by the basic design of the CPU. Information is coded and processed internally in bits, ones and zeros, represented by electronic switches being turned on and off. The CPU employs special sets of these switches, known as registers, for processing information. The register size is what determines word size in a computer.

Currently there are microcomputers with eight, 16, and 32 bit word sizes. It is a safe generalization to say that computing power increases significantly with word size, although there are some exceptions to this. In general we are seeing a trend toward increasing computing power at decreasing cost so that today's microcomputers exceed the power of minicomputers and even mainframe computers of just a few years ago.

A special CPU register is employed for handling memory locations. This *address register* is generally larger than the CPU word length, and its size determines the maximum internal memory size that the CPU can directly address. Since the memory addresses are represented in the address register as a binary number, the maximum memory size will be a power of two. Memory size is normally measured in terms of K where 1K equals 1,024 (two raised to the tenth power) or in units of M (1,024 times 1,024 or approximately one million). Memory is usually measured in units of *bytes*. A byte is a sequence of eight bits, which is used to code a character. Thus we read about computers with 640 K bytes of random access memory (RAM), and others with two megabytes (or MB) of memory.

Memory size is important to the microcomputer user since it limits the power and capacity to run very large programs efficiently. Many modern database software packages require a minimum of 256 K and sometimes more in order to run. This means that the older eight bit machines cannot handle programs of this size even if they could be translated into their CPU's machine language.

Beyond the minimum memory required, many packages can use additional memory to advantage, for example giving faster response. Recently there have been schemes developed to get around the memory address limitations of some popular CPUs (notably the Intel 8088 family). These extended memory systems are particularly useful for handling large spreadsheets and may also enhance database software performance.

The use of high speed internal memory to emulate a disk drive (RAM disk) is another way to significantly increase the performance of database software. Internal memory can be accessed in the order of one hundred nanoseconds (billionths of a second), while external disk access requires time measured in the tens of milliseconds (thousandths of a second). By copying some files to a RAM disk (for example the index files for a database) response times can be reduced significantly.

Another factor in the CPU design that has a direct bearing on performance is the *clock rate*. The basic operations of the CPU are performed in a regularly timed series of actions. The rate at which these are done is determined by the clock rate or cycle time of the CPU. Clock rates are measured in megaHerz (MHz) or millions of cycles per second. Clock rates of six to 20 MHz are common today, and the trend is to increasing speeds.

Other things being equal, an increase in a CPU's clock rate will produce a proportional increase in its processing performance. Applications that involve significant input and output (disk accessing, and so on) will not be speeded up as much as those that are CPU intensive.

MEMORY

Data to be processed and instructions for processing the data are both stored in the computer's internal memory. Memory components in microcomputers are microelectronic switching circuits (semiconductor memory). The performance of the computer depends not only on the CPU speed, but also on the access time of the memory chips. The memory in a computer must be capable of responding in the time for one cycle of the CPU. With a clock rate of five MHz this computes to 200 nanoseconds.

The general purpose internal memory in a computer is often referred to as RAM (random access memory). Read/write memory might be a better name for it to distinguish it from another form of internal memory called ROM (read only memory). RAM is generally volatile—its contents are lost when the computer is turned off. ROM is nonvolatile and is used to store values that are needed on a permanent basis. A common example of read only memory use is the Basic Input/Output System (BIOS), which handles the chores of starting up the computer when it is turned on and loads the rest of the operating system from disk.

Another variable in RAM chips is static versus dynamic. Most current memory components are dynamic due to the fact that they are cheaper to produce. Dynamic memory needs to be continuously refreshed in order to retain its contents. This refreshing is handled by the memory circuitry and is totally transparent to the user or the software.

Memory chips are easy to spot when looking inside a computer with the cover off. They are the small ones lined up neatly in rows of eight or nine. When you find nine chips per row that is an indication that the system you are looking at uses *parity* checking for its memory. Parity involves the adding of a ninth bit to the standard eight bit byte and setting or resetting (storing a one or a zero) in the ninth bit so that there will always be an even number of ones (even parity) or an odd number of ones (odd parity). When a bit is accidentally flipped (changed from a one to a zero or from a zero to a one) the computer will detect the error.

INPUT/OUTPUT

The third essential set of components in a computer are the input and output ports. It must be possible for the user to enter data and instructions, and for the computer to respond in some way. These communication processes require specialized circuitry. Examples of devices that are commonly employed only for input are the keyboard, joystick, light pen, and mouse. Examples of output devices include the CRT screen, printer, plotter, and speakers. Devices that can function for both input and output include magnetic disk and tape drives.

There are two basic modes of communication used by computers: serial and parallel. Serial communications devices send and receive information in a stream of bits. To send one byte in serial mode involves sending each of the eight bits on one wire in sequence. The receiver would then reconstruct the byte after receiving all eight of the bits. The kind of serial communications most commonly found on microcomputers is asynchronous. In order to tell when a byte has begun and when it ends when transmitting a stream of bits, the sending and receiving systems must either be synchronized or, for asynchronous communication, there must be additional signal components to indicate the starting and stopping of each byte. We commonly find serial communications systems using a start bit and a stop bit, and seven bits for an ASCII character, and one bit for parity, making a total of ten bits per byte. Synchronous communication requires more elaborate (and expensive) circuitry to control the timing.

Parallel communications devices operate by sending and receiving each bit of a byte on a separate wire so that each byte arrives intact at the same time. Printers are a common example of devices that often employ parallel communication.

Parallel devices are less expensive than serial devices, but must be connected by a relatively short cable for reliable communication (10 to 12 feet or shorter). Serial devices may be separated by as much as 2,000 feet.

In order to connect devices to your computer you must have the appropriate electronics circuitry (often in the form of plug-in adapter boards) and appropriate connectors. For serial communications there is a standard connector known variously as a DB25 or RS232C connector. Actually the plug or socket is a DB25, and the standard that specifies how the 25 pins are to be used is the RS232C standard.

In practice, the various manufacturers of computers and peripheral equipment follow the standard with varying degrees of vigor. Furthermore, there are two standards, one for devices that primarily receive data (DTE or data terminal equipment) and one for devices that primarily send data (DCE or data communication equipment).

Parallel communications connections are not as well standardized as serial connections, although for printers the Centronics 36 pin connector is common.

STORAGE

External storage of programs and data can employ a variety of media and associated hardware. By far the most common form of external storage for microcomputers is the magnetic disk. There are, however, several other methods for storing data.

Magnetic Disk

Magnetic disk storage comes in several varieties: flexible or floppy disks in 8- , 5¼- , 3½-inch sizes and varying formats and capacities for each size; fixed hard disks (also known as Winchester disks); removable hard disks; and Bernoulli technology disk packs. Floppy disks are the common medium for software distribution. They are convenient for storage of small data files, but for most database applications they suffer from too low capacity, slow access, and media wear and degradation with time and usage. Floppy disk recording densities continue to increase, and it is now possible to store several megabytes on a floppy. They might be considered for a small database application.

Hard disks are more commonly used for database applications due to their greater capacity, faster access times, and greater reliability. Capacities ranging from 10 MB to a few hundred MB are available, although many users now consider 20 or 30 MB to be a more reasonable lower limit, since the cost differential is small.

The main problem with a fixed hard disk is that it is fixed. When it is full, you have to either take something off the disk or buy another one. Backing up files on a fixed disk also presents problems in that it requires some other media to record and hold the backup copies.

Removable hard disks answer the capacity problem in the way floppy disks do—you can have any number of disks on your shelf, so storage is unlimited. You can only access a portion of the total at one time. With removable hard disks that portion can be 20 MB or more, enough for many microcomputer database systems. With dual drives the removable hard disks can be used for backup also. Bernoulli technology is another approach to removable high capacity disk storage. This technique uses flexible disks in a rigid cartridge with the read/write head floating on a cushion of air over the surface of the disks. This medium offers most of the advantages of removable hard disks and is very robust; however, the drives are more costly, and the disks are more subject to wear. Disk controller circuitry is required in addition to the drives for all of these options.

Optical Storage

Optical-laser media offer possibilities for inhouse database production in two ways: as a source of published records to be transferred to the local database and as an alternative to magnetic media for the storage of the local database. An example of the first application is the Bibliofile system, which provides access to about three million MARC book records on four CD ROM (Compact Disk-Read Only Memory). The use of optical media for local database storage will generally require write and possibly erase capabilities. This technology is evolving rapidly so it can be expected to be competitive soon with magnetic media for large files.

Optical-laser disks, such as CD ROM and the larger format videodisks, involve the mass production of copies through a mastering process. Several recording formats are used; for example, CD ROM uses digital recording methods. Other methods used for recording digital data include encoding it in television video format. The video recording methods allow the mixing of digital, video, and audio content on the same disk with a higher capacity than for digital recording. Standards are being developed so that disks from various sources will be hardware compatible (that is they can be used with the same disk player and controller circuitry).

CD ROM makes use of the technology developed for the compact audio disk. This helps bring the cost down as there is a much greater market for the audio media. CD ROM is being used extensively for the publication of commercial databases and database subsets. These offer an alternative to searching databases online.

The optical digital disk, which uses a laser to directly write to the disk so that it can be immediately read, has a more direct application to inhouse database development. This system offers an alternative to magnetic recording for the storage of database files. There are several methods used for direct recording with a laser. In contrast to CD ROM, which records data in a spiral track, the optical digital disks record in concentric tracks as is done in magnetic disks. The result is a lower capacity than with the CD ROM, but with significantly faster access times. Optical digital disks fall into two major types: erasable and nonerasable.

For many database applications the inability to erase the contents of the disk would be considered an advantage. For very volatile files this would definitely be a problem. The non-erasable technology is commonly referred to as WORM (write-once, read many times or read mostly, or, if used for archiving, read maybe). The WORM technology is relatively more developed than is the erasable media. Recording is done by burning a spot on the recording surface with a laser, or permanently altering the light reflecting properties in some other way (for example, using the laser to produce a small blister on the surface, or to change the crystal structure of the material).

Erasable optical media are now available commercially at competitive costs on a per megabyte basis. Magneto-optical recording appears to be the most viable approach to erasable optical storage. While this technology records by altering the magnetic orientation of the recording medium as does magnetic recording, lasers are used in both writing and reading. To write, a laser beam heats a spot to a temperature where the magnetic material in the recording surface will become reoriented in a magnetic field. Reading is done with another lower intensity polarized laser beam. The magnetized spots alter the angle of polarization of the reflected beam, making it possible to detect the spots. Capacities of about 800 megabytes are currently available with magneto-optical drives. These media offer many of the same advantages as magnetic disks, but with higher capacity and longer media life. At this point the typical inhouse database developer will probably choose magnetic media, but the optical media bear watching and can be expected to become competitive for these applications before long.

PRINTERS

Most inhouse database systems will need printing capabilities. The options for printers range from the cheap to the very expensive, depending on speed, print quality, flexibility, and durability. Common printer types are dot matrix (impact, thermal, ink jet, and laser), and formed letter. There are some special considerations regarding printers that arise in the design of an inhouse database system.

Depending on the kinds of reports to be produced and their intended use, different printer characteristics will be needed. If, for instance, you intend to publish listings from the database, a letter quality printer will be needed. Some of the database software will allow the use of printer control codes in formatted reports in order to turn on and off special effects, such as italics, bold, underline printing, and to change fonts if your printer will support this.

If a great deal of printing is expected, the durability of the printer will be an important consideration. If it will be used in a public area the noise level should be low. Special forms will require a forms tractor that can adjust to the width of the form.

MODEMS

In order to access remote databases (to download records, for example) or for remote users to access your system, a modem will be needed. A modem is a device that converts the computer's digital signal to analog form for transmission over telephone lines and then converts a received signal from analog to digital. Modems come in internal and external forms. The internal type is in the form of a card that plugs into an expansion slot of the computer. These internal modems have a modular telephone jack, which allows for the direct connection of the modem to the telephone system. The modem card draws its power from the computer's internal power supply.

An external modem is connected to the computer by means of a serial communications port, which means that you may have to add a serial communication card to your computer if it does not already have a serial port. You will have to provide a source of power for the external modem, which requires one more electrical outlet.

The other major variable in modems is the communications rate. Common rates are 300, 1,200, 2,400, and 9,600 bits per second. For alphanumeric data this translates to 30, 120, 240, and 960 characters per second (the ASCII code uses seven bits per byte and one bit each is used for parity, start bit and stop bit, making ten bits for each character).

To make use of the modem you will also need a communications program. Some of the integrated database/file manager packages include communications functions as part of the package (for example, the Sci-Mate system's Searcher module). Otherwise you will need a separate communications program. Most are written for the Hayes Smart Modem. Most modems do use the Hayes command set, sometimes with additions and/or changes. Some seem to be more compatible than others.

MULTIUSER SYSTEMS

Most microcomputer systems are single user systems. For many applications, however, more than one person may need to use an inhouse database. The simplest approach to multiple users is to take turns with a single user system. When there are multiple users, it is often the case that some users will be authorized to enter and modify data while others will only have read access, and all users may not have access to all data. Password security is normally used to control access. Many single user systems do not address this need.

Contention for the machine and/or geographic distance may argue for multiple work stations. One technically simple approach is to distribute multiple copies of a single user system, each with a copy of the database and the retrieval software. (Additional copies of the software will usually have to be purchased because most use agreements do not allow making multiple copies.) This approach also introduces the problem of keeping all copies of the database current. Making all changes at a central location and distributing updated versions on a regular schedule is probably the safest approach.

Multiple copies of the same database works best with relatively static databases because it is not feasible to distribute updated databases too frequently. Distribution on CD ROM may be a viable alternative for large databases because the data cannot be altered at the distributed sites.

When local input at more than one location is needed, a central database with remote access makes it easier to maintain data integrity. Two approaches are possible for multiuser access to a microcomputer-based central database: a single CPU multiuser system or a Local Area Network (LAN).

Multiuser systems on minicomputers and mainframes have been standard for many years. More recently, multiuser operating systems have become available for some microcomputers. Examples include UNIX, PICK, and AMOS. With these operating systems, a single CPU supports the processing of several users, ranging from three to ten or more depending on the power of the CPU and the efficiency of the operating system. Each user needs only an inexpensive dumb terminal to connect to the central CPU.

Unfortunately, there are not many software packages suitable for textual databases that run on multiuser systems. Those that do are frequently more costly and more complex to use. Some suitable multiuser software packages are mentioned in Chapter 7.

With Local Area Networks (LANs) each user station is a microcomputer, which performs much of the processing locally. Files, printers, and other peripherals may be shared among all the computers that are attached to the network. A LAN usually has one computer that is dedicated to a *file server* role—that is, it provides access to all the other machines and files on the network. In addition, a LAN requires cables to link all machines to the network, LAN interface cards for each microcomputer, and special LAN software. The LAN software interacts with the operating systems of the computers on the network, intercepting disk access requests and directing them to the file server.

Not all software for inhouse databases will work on a LAN. Special features such as those that insure data integrity are necessary. Multiuser systems and LAN-based systems must guard against the simultaneous updating of the same record by more than one user. File, record, and/or data element locking features are necessary in both options for multiuser software.

BACKUP AND SECURITY

Backing up files should be a regular part of maintaining an inhouse database. Files can become corrupted, lightning may strike, or your building may burn down. The data files constitute the largest single investment of your database system and are the most difficult to replace if lost. The relatively modest cost of backup hardware and storage media and the time required to do regular backups is cheap insurance against disaster.

File Backup Options

Options for file backup include (in order of increasing cost):

- floppy disks
- tape cartridge
- removable hard disk cartridge
- Bernouli disk cartridge
- WORM optical disk

Erasable optical disks could be used as well, but WORM makes more sense for backup because it cannot be erased.

Most microcomputer systems will have one or two floppy disk drives, so this option involves no extra hardware costs. This method is the most tedious and time consuming, and the flexible disks are vulnerable to accidental erasure or damage. Backup software splits large files across multiple disks.

Tape backup systems are available in several formats. Two methods of hard disk backup on tape are *streaming tape copying* and *file by file* copying. With streaming tape, a mirror image of the entire disk is made, including sectors blanked out by the operating systems due to disk defects. One potential problem with the streaming tape system is that if the hard disk is damaged and replaced with a new one, the bad sectors will be in different locations, and the disk image will not copy to the new disk. This kind of backup will protect against accidental erasure of data, but not always against damage to the disk.

File by file tape backup allows either wholesale copying of the entire disk or selected files (as is the case with floppy disk backup). This gets around the previously mentioned problem of hard disk replacement. Tape cartridges and cassettes of varying capacity are available to efficiently backup most hard disks. Many of the tape drives are designed to fit in the space of a half height 5¼-inch floppy drive.

Alpha Micro markets a backup system called VIDEOTRAX, which uses standard videotape cassettes and videotape player/recorders. This system offers a convenient and low cost storage medium for backup. The system can be programmed to automatically backup the hard disk at a time when the computer is not being used. Up to 80 Megabytes can be recorded on a standard two-hour cassette.

Cartridge disk systems offer fast file by file backup and can also serve as the primary storage medium. Capacities for the removable hard disks and Bernouli disks are in the range of ten to 20 megabytes, so a large hard disk will require more than one cartridge to back it up. Most inhouse databases will fit on a 20 megabyte drive.

Write-once optical disk technology offers high capacity storage in a relatively stable medium. The fact that the data cannot be erased is a definite advantage for backup purposes. Costs may be prohibitive at present, but prices are expected to fall significantly. This option is one to keep in mind as the technology matures. As with cartridge disks, WORM could also serve for the primary database storage.

Power Conditioning

Another aspect of backup and system security concerns the quality and availability of electrical power. The electrical power to your computer is subject to three types of problems that can cause unexplained errors, data loss, file damage, or circuit damage. These problems are voltage surges or spikes, high frequency noise, and partial or total power loss (brownouts or blackouts).

Transient voltage spikes of several thousand volts are not uncommon in unconditioned electrical lines. Electrical storms can cause massive voltage surges that can severely damage the electronic circuits in your computer and peripherals. High frequency noise (variations from the standard 60 cycle or 50 cycle sine wave) can also cause data errors.

Many database systems are particularly sensitive to power loss when files are open. A loss of power for only a second or less can cause file corruption and possible hardware damage. Power conditioning equipment is available to deal with each of these problems. Surge suppression or spike suppression devices protect against transient voltage jumps; filter circuits remove noise; constant voltage transformers correct for voltage drops experienced in a brownout; and standby power supplies and uninterruptible power supplies provide reserve power from rechargeable batteries. The computer system thus can be shut down gracefully in the event of a long outage or can continue to operate through a short outage.

Power conditioning systems generally offer protection against more than one problem. Inexpensive line conditioners often combine surge suppression and noise filtering. Constant voltage power supplies include surge suppression and filtering also. Standby power supplies (SPS) of uninterruptible power supplies (UPS) generally protect against all three types of problems.

The difference between standby and uninterruptible power supplies is that the standby systems are offline and only switch online when the voltage drops below a set amount. The uninterruptible power supply is always online, providing continuous, regulated, noise free power. Significant variables in SPS and UPS units include

- capacity, measured in volt amperes (VA) and sometimes translated into backup time in minutes at specified loads,
- wave form (sine wave or square wave; square wave systems tend to be less expensive but some computers cannot operate with them),
- switching time (for SPS), measured in miliseconds.

The telephone line provides another route by which electrical storms can damage your computer, if you have a modem installed or attached. Surge suppression devices are available for modems as well as for power lines.

FURTHER READINGS

Abelson, P.W. "The Revolution in Computers and Electronics." *Science* 215 (12 February 1982): 751–753.

Boraiko, Allen A. "The Chips." *National Geographic* 162 (October 1982): 421–476.

Branscomb, Louis M. "Electronic Computers: An Overview." *Science* 215 (12 February 1982): 755–760.

Browning, Dave. "Data Managers and LANs." *PC Tech Journal* 5 (May 1987): 54–70.

Burton, Paul F. and Petrie, J. Howard. *The Librarian's Guide to Microcomputers for Information Management.* Norfolk (U.K.): Van Nostrand Reinhold (UK), 1986.

Chen, Ching-chih and Bressler, Stacey E., eds. *Microcomputers in Libraries.* New York: Neal-Schuman, 1982.

Davis, Charles H. and Rush, James E. *Guide to Information Science.* Westport, Conn.: Greenwood Press, 1979.

Lambert, Steve and Ropiequet, Suzanne, eds. *CD/ROM: The New Papyrus.* Redmond, Wash.: MicroSoft Press, 1986.

Lefkon, Dick. "A LAN Primer." *Byte* 12 (July 1987): 147–154.

Meadow, Charles T. and Tedesco, Albert S. *Telecommunications for Management.* New York: McGraw Hill, 1985.

McQueen, Judy and Boss, Richard. *Videodisc and Optical Disk Technologies and Their Applications in Libraries, 1986 Update.* Chicago: American Library Association, 1986.

3

Search Features and File Structures

Retrieving information from a database involves identifying a set of documents or items whose members in some way match or are similar to the query or statement of information need. This involves two aspects of retrieval systems design that will determine the power and capability of the system: the query (command) language and the matching (searching) process. These are based on a third factor—the file structure used (the manner in which the records are organized in the file). These factors directly affect response time and storage requirements.

Software packages for textual databases vary in the power and flexibility of searching, but they generally provide features similar to those that have been developed over the last 20 years on the large commercial database systems. These features are to a large extent dictated by the nature of textual databases and the ways in which the databases are used.

WHY TEXTUAL DATABASES ARE UNIQUE

As mentioned in Chapter 1, textual databases are of three main types: bibliographic, full text, and referral. In turn, these types may refer to or include a wide variety of materials, such as journal articles, books, audiovisual materials, correspondence, memos, or the proverbial recipe file. While the applications and the information content vary widely, there are characteristics shared by most textual databases that set them apart from other types of databases.

Alphanumeric Characters

Most of the information in textual databases is composed of alphabetic characters. Fields such as title, author, abstracts, and citations contain mostly words, not numbers. Even fields that include numbers (page numbers, for instance) treat the numeric information as character strings rather than as numbers to be used in computations.

129,702

25

The preponderance of alphabetic information sets these databases apart from most databases in an office environment. Few computational powers are needed in software designed for textual databases; the strength of information retrieval software must lie in its ability to manipulate character strings and offer special search features that incorporate grammatical structure. These features (such as word proximity searching) are discussed later in this chapter.

Size

Textual databases often are larger than other types of databases. Databases that refer to a body of literature or provide access to complete texts tend to grow because new records are added, while older ones retain their usefulness. Information is seldom removed from textual databases as it might be, for example, from an inventory database.

Field Characteristics

Records in textual databases usually have many fields, but each field tends to vary widely in length. The title field in a bibliographic database, for example, might have to accommodate a range of lengths from just a few characters up to several hundred. Similarly, paragraphs in a full text database or memos in a memo database may range from a single sentence to hundreds of words. Software that can only handle fixed length fields results in wasted storage space because the length must be set to hold the longest value anticipated. Many fixed length software packages have an upper limit to field length (often 255 characters, sometimes shorter). This upper limit is often too short to accommodate the information required in some fields in a textual database.

Although the length and values in each field tend to vary widely from record to record, the same fields are usually present in each record. The fields needed for standard bibliographic description, for example, vary little once the database designer sets them up. Fields such as author, title, and publication year are consistently found in almost all records.

Repeating Values

One of the characteristics of most textual databases is the need for multiple values in a given field. The number of authors in a bibliographic file, for example, might range from zero to several, or the number of ingredients in a recipe may vary from one to many. Multiple subject descriptors are almost always assigned. Although values repeat in these fields, the number of repetitions is unpredictable from one record to the next. Each value in these fields is typically of equal importance, however, and for retrieval purposes needs to be treated in the same way. Users will want equal access to every subject descriptor in a database to satisfy different queries. They do not want to know that a particular subject is the first, second, or third subject in a record.

Database systems that allow only one value per field force the system designer to make compromises that generally result in wasted space and poorer retrieval performance. You might, for example, decide that your bibliographic records will include up to three authors. With a single value per field you would have to create three fields, such as AU1, AU2, and AU3. This will waste space for those records with fewer than three and will not deal with those with more than three. Perhaps more objectionable is the impact on retrieval capability. To find records in which Smith was an author or coauthor it will be necessary to search three fields rather than one.

Multiple Access Points

Because users are typically searching for an unknown set of items rather than selecting known items, the nature of the retrieval process is complex in textual databases. One aspect of this complexity is the number of ways of specifying the records to be retrieved. In many cases the user does not know how many records will be found that will satisfy his or her query, and the records that are retrieved typically are satisfying to varying degrees.

One way to increase the quality of the searches is to provide as many ways to search for records as possible—i.e., to allow retrieval on all fields that might be useful. In many applications all or nearly all of the fields will provide useful access to the database contents. Moreover, access to a field will be enhanced to the extent that the query can include fragments or partial contents (key words from titles, truncated names, and so on).

Complex Queries

The complexities of records and fields in textual databases is equaled by the need to be able to formulate complex queries. Essentially, what is required is the capacity to combine concepts or clues in logical relationships and to modify the query based on intermediate results. Information needs are often somewhat vague and ill-defined, and information that is retrieved varies in usefulness. Logical flexibility will help to cope with these kinds of needs. Several ways of retrieving the appropriate information are found to varying degrees in most textual database systems. These are discussed in detail later in the chapter.

Inverted Indexes

The fact that textual databases are commonly searched by many access points means that it is not practical for the system to store the records in a sequence determined by a single retrieval key. Generally, the sequence of records in the file is of little consequence for search and retrieval. A specified order may be important to the user at output (for example, retrieved records arranged alphabetically by author). This is done by a sort option used at the time the output report is generated.

Software for textual databases commonly arranges the records in the order in which they are added to the file. That is, the file simply grows by adding new records to the end. The resulting file is a sequential file (often referred to in this context as the linear file). Figure 3.1 shows the first two records in a linear file of a bibliographic database.

If there are only a few records in the database, the database can be searched by examining each character in turn in each field in each record in the entire sequential file. For example, to find records containing the term "construction" in Figure 3.1, the system would begin with record number 001. Starting with the first field (AN), the computer would scan each character in turn until it found the character string CONSTRUCTION in the abstract. The system would report to the user that this record contains the desired word. Depending on the software in use, the system would then either immediately display the retrieved record or place it in a set and continue searching sequentially through the file. As you can imagine, this approach quickly becomes impractical. Logical combinations (e.g., CONSTRUCTION and TESTING) are especially time-consuming.

To speed retrieval and allow more search capabilities, nearly all of the information retrieval systems today create inverted indexes. Inverted indexes (also called dictionary files or alphabetic indexes) extract the searchable words or phrases from the linear file and list

FIGURE 3.1   Records in a Linear File

AN   001
TI   The Three Little Pigs
AU   Mother Goose
PU   Wee Press
CY   London
PY   1899
AB   Real-life testing of house construction methods. Demonstrates
      advantages and disadvantages of straw, sticks, and bricks.
DE   Swine, Miniature; Residential Architecture
ID   Wolf, Big Bad

AN   002
TI   The House That Jack Built
AU   Mother Goose
PU   Children's Book Company Inc.
CY   New York
PY   1985
AB   Construction tips for novices. Describes occupants
      of Jack's house.
DE   Residential Architecture; Animals in fiction
ID   Jack

---

them in a separate alphabetically ordered file with pointers back to the appropriate unit record in the linear file. Figure 3.2 shows part of an inverted index file. This index file provides rapid access to individual items.

Organization of Inverted Indexes. Inverted index files can be organized and searched in several different ways. One of the simplest and most common ways to organize the index file is to use an *ordered sequential* file structure. In an ordered sequential file, the extracted searchable terms are stored on a direct access device (such as a disk drive) in alphabetical order. Such a file is efficiently searched using the binary search method.

The binary search method searches ordered files by first examining the middle value. If the middle value is not the value sought, the top or bottom half of the file is ignored depending on whether the middle item was less than or greater than the search key. This is repeated with the remaining half and so on, with the yet to be searched portion of the file being reduced by half each time. A file of 65,000 items can be searched with no more than 16 comparisons this way, as opposed to 65,000 comparisons for a straight sequential scan.

Figure 3.2   Inverted Index File

VALUE	RECORD	FIELD	POSITION
1899	001	py	01
1985	002	py	01
advantages	001	ab	08
animals	002	de	03
animals in fiction	002	de	03-05
architecture	001	de	04
	002	de	02
bad	001	id	03
big	001	id	02
bricks	001	ab	15
built	002	ti	05
construction	001	ab	05
	002	ab	01
demonstrates	001	ab	07
describes	002	ab	05
disadvantages	001	ab	10
fiction	002	de	05
house	001	ab	04
	002	ti	02
	002	ab	09
jack	002	ti	04
	002	id	01
jack's	002	ab	08
life	001	ab	01
little	001	ti	03
methods	001	ab	06
miniature	001	de	02
mother goose	001	au	01
	002	au	01
novices	002	ab	04
occupants	002	ab	06
pigs	001	ti	04
real-time	001	ab	01
residential	001	de	03
	002	de	01
residential architecture	001	de	03-04
	002	de	01-02
.	.	.	
.	.	.	
.	.	.	
wolf, big bad	001	id	01-03

Inverted file structures greatly speed up searching because when a user searches for a term, the system goes to the inverted index rather than scanning the linear file. Some systems maintain a separate inverted index for each searchable field, others interfile terms from all fields. The amount of information included in the inverted index varies, sometimes according to user specified criteria. A typical inverted file, as shown in Figure 3.2, includes the accession number of each record that contains the term, the fields where the term is found in each record, and the placement of each term in each field (e.g., the fifth word in the title field of the five hundredth record). The impact of this information on search capabilities is discussed later in this chapter.

Using the inverted index, the retrieval system first reports the number of records that contain a search term (called *hits* or *postings*). The accession numbers for the records that satisfy a given search request are put into a separate numbered list called a *set*. Sets are created for each search term or for each search statement. Not until the searcher enters a display command does the system use the accession numbers stored in the set to access the linear file records.

Parsing. As you design your database, you will decide what fields will be included in the records. You will also decide which fields are to be searchable and designated for inclusion in the inverted files. One of the most important decisions at this stage is how each field will be processed for the inverted indexes. The database creator has some control over this processing by deciding how each field will be *parsed* by the computer. *Parsing* is the process of identifying how each field will be separated out of the linear file for entry into the inverted index. How a field is parsed is important because it greatly affects how the words or terms in a record can be searched.

Three automatic parsing options are generally available, although the options open to you vary with the software selected. If software offers you all three options, each field in a record can be parsed according to what makes the most sense for the kind of data stored in it.

Word parsing (word indexing) is commonly chosen for subject related fields such as the title field, abstract field, or full text fields that do not use controlled vocabulary. With word parsing, each individual word is usually defined as any string of letters and/or numbers bounded by blanks and/or punctuation. When parsing a word indexed field, the system would create a separate entry in the inverted index each time a word is encountered. Thus the title *Developing Computer-Based Library Systems* would have five separate alphabetically arranged entries in the inverted index: BASED, COMPUTER, DEVELOPING, LIBRARY, and SYSTEMS. Some software counts the hyphen as a meaningful character instead of as the beginning or end of a word. In such a system, this title would have only four entries in a word parsed inverted index: COMPUTER-BASED, DEVELOPING, LIBRARY, and SYSTEMS.

Most retrieval software packages allow a list of trivial or non-informative words (*stop words*) that are not included in the inverted indexes. Stop words typically include prepositions, such as of and with, articles such as an and the, and conjunctions such as and, or, and but. Some software comes with a preset list of stop words that the database designer cannot alter. Other software will allow you to designate your own stop words.

When the computer creates the inverted index, it checks the stop word list and does not make an entry for any word on the list. *In Search of Excellence* would have only two entries in the inverted index of most systems: EXCELLENCE and SEARCH. Many systems retain word placement information about stop words, however, so the system would note that EXCELLENCE was the fourth word in the title and SEARCH was the second word.

Phrase parsing (phrase indexing) is usually used for controlled fields where a human indexer has indicated that the words in a phrase go together as a *bound* phrase. Phrase parsed entries in the inverted index generally include all spaces and punctuation. The computer software can detect where one phrase ends and another begins because the index terms are marked with special delimiters.

Phrase parsing keeps bound terms together, but it affects searching. The entire phrase must be searched in order to retrieve the desired records. Individual words in a multi-word descriptor phrase are not accessible for searching, and authors cannot be searched by their first name only if the field is indexed this way.

The author field is often phrase parsed. Author names in their inverted form (last, first, middle) can be searched based on the last name and as much of the first and middle as needed to differentiate one author from another.

Combination parsed fields (*double posted*) are both word parsed and phrase parsed. Bound phrases are kept together, but they are also separated at spaces and punctuation. This approach is typically used in the descriptor and identifier fields where there are bound (*precoordinated*) phrases, but where individual words are also meaningful (e.g., PROGRAMMING LANGUAGES and STRUCTURED

FIGURE 3.3   How Records Will Be Parsed

AN   001
TI   The Three Little Pigs
AU   Mother Goose
PU   Wee Press
CY   London
PY   1899
AB   Real-life testing of house construction methods. Demonstrates
     advantages and disadvantages of straw, sticks, and bricks.
DE   Swine, Miniature; Residential Architecture
ID   Wolf, Big Bad

AN   002
TI   The House That Jack Built
AU   Mother Goose
PU   Children's Book Company Inc.
CY   New York
PY   1985
AB   Construction tips for novices. Describes occupants
     of Jack's house.
DE   Residential Architecture; Animals in fiction
ID   Jack

PROGRAMMING could both be retrieved by the query term
PROGRAMMING).

Double posting is helpful to the user because it retains the
intellectual decisions involved in creating a bound descriptor, yet it
allows individual words to be searched when a user may not know the
correct form of a bound term or when a broader search is wanted (as in
the case of PROGRAMMING in the previous example). Combination
parsing allows the most flexibility for the searcher, but also creates
the longest inverted index and consequently uses the most storage
space on the computer. Figure 3.3 illustrates how the records were
parsed to create the inverted index shown in Figure 3.2.

SEARCH FEATURES

As mentioned earlier, parsing decisions have a direct impact on
how a database can be searched. Word parsed fields can be searched
by individual words, phrase parsed fields by complete phrases, but

fields that are double posted can be searched by either words or phrases.

The growth and development of the online information industry has produced a high level of expectation on the part of today's information system users. Users' expectations have been elevated even more by experiences with a variety of well-designed microcomputer software that takes advantage of the better user interface capabilities provided by microcomputers.

Computer based retrieval systems usually have searching features that provide flexibility in searching regardless of how the fields were parsed. These features include truncation, the ability to view the inverted index on the screen, proximity searching, Boolean logic, set building and stepwise refinement, range searching, comparison searching, and the ability to specify the fields to be searched.

Most of these features are found in almost all publicly available online systems that provide access to textual databases. They have developed into a de facto standard for search capabilities for all textual databases, whether they are publicly available or inhouse. The manner in which these features are implemented differs from online system to system. The extent to which they are provided on microcomputer software varies widely. The search features discussed below can be considered the standards that are desirable to some degree for nearly every textual database.

Truncation

Most systems allow the searcher to use term truncation to search for all terms or phrases that begin with the same character stem. This is usually indicated to the system by a special truncation symbol. Thus, putting a truncation symbol after the stem LIBRAR will find entries in the inverted index under LIBRARY, LIBRARIANSHIP, LIBRARY AUTOMATION, and so on. (The truncation symbol varies from system to system, some common ones are ?, #, *, and /).

Other variations in truncation are found in some systems. Left hand truncation is not common, but can be useful in certain situations such as in a chemical database. More common variations include the ability to specify the maximum length of the term as well as the stem (e.g., to retrieve DRUG or DRUGS but not DRUGGIST, DRUGSTORE, and so on.). The imbedded ambiguity marker is sometimes called a *wild card* character, particularly where a character for character substitution is required (e.g., WOM*N). Some systems also provide an internal truncation symbol that will allow a variable number of characters, so that LAB*R will retrieve LABOR, LABOUR, and any other word (such as LABRADOR) beginning with LAB and ending with R.

Truncation is especially valuable for phrase indexed fields because it will allow a searcher to retrieve records without knowing the complete phrase. Truncated searching for the author LANCASTER will retrieve all records that contain an author with the last name of Lancaster. If truncation is available, the searcher does not have to enter the spacing, punctuation, or initials exactly right as required by phrase parsing because they all come after the truncation symbol.

Index Display

Most retrieval systems allow the searcher to view parts of the alphabetic inverted index. By looking at the inverted index, the searcher can see what words or phrases are available for searching, see the many term variations that occur (especially in uncontrolled fields), and find the exact phrase and format that must be entered to search a phrase indexed field. This can help eliminate false drops caused by truncation or key word searching.

In addition to displaying a segment of the alphabetized list of terms, many systems show the number of postings for each term. This aids in search strategy development. Some systems allow browsing up and down the list, some permit the searcher to specify the range to be displayed (e.g., from bird to butterfly), and others display a fixed number of terms on either side of a specified term.

Proximity Searching

Word proximity searching is an especially powerful feature for searching word parsed fields. Proximity searching allows a searcher to *post-coordinate* phrases from word indexed fields, such as titles or abstracts. This is made possible by means of the positional information that is stored with each entry in the inverted index. This positional information indicates the field and the location within the field for each term. A searcher can ask, for example, for the word LIBRARY immediately followed by the word AUTOMATION in a word indexed or double posted field. The system will use the positional information to reconstruct the phrase even though each word is entered separately in the inverted index.

Proximity features vary among systems. Some typical capabilities include the ability to specify words adjacent to each other, words with a specified number of intervening words (in a specified order or independent of order), words in the same sentence, words in the same paragraph, or words in the same field.

Boolean Logic

One of the common means of facilitating complex query formulation is with the use of the Boolean operators AND, OR, and NOT. These correspond to the set operations of intersection, union, and complement. These three operators are found in almost all textual database systems in some form or another.

The AND operator narrows a search by producing a set whose elements are common to both component sets. For example, the expression CATS AND FLEAS will operate on the set of records identified by the term CATS and the set of records identified by the term FLEAS. The result will be a set of records identified by *both* terms.

The OR operator expands a search by producing a set whose elements are found in either component set. For example, the expression CATS OR DOGS will produce a set whose elements are identified by *either* of the terms (or both).

The NOT operator produces a set whose elements are not identified by the specified term. In most systems NOT is equivalent to AND NOT. The expression CATS NOT FLEAS will produce a set of records identified by the term CATS, but not identified by the term FLEAS. In some systems NOT may be used as a prefix operator. NOT CATS will produce a set made up of all records in the database not identified by the term CATS.

These Boolean operations are conveniently illustrated by the use of Venn diagrams. Figure 3.4 illustrates the three basic Boolean operations. The rectangle is meant to represent the entire database; the circles, the component single term sets; and the crosshatched areas, the resulting set produced by the operation.

Logical operators generally have an established order of precedence so that expressions involving more than one operator will be unambiguous. The most common order is NOT, AND, and OR.

Most systems that support multioperator query statements also support parenthetical grouping as a means of controlling the order of operations. Expressions within parentheses are operated on by the system before any operations outside the parentheses. Thus, the expression (CATS OR DOGS) AND (FLEAS OR TICKS) will first produce a pets set and a pest set, then produce the AND combination.

FIGURE 3.4   Venn Diagrams Illustrating Boolean Operators

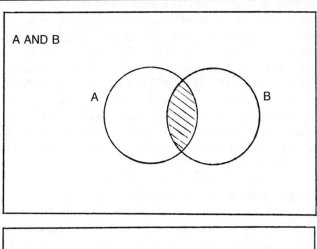

A AND B

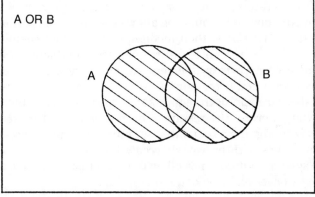

A OR B

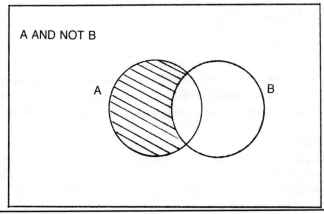

A AND NOT B

Given the order of precedence above, the query without the parentheses would give different (and unwanted) results.

Use of more than one level of parentheses, *nesting,* is allowed in some systems. Such nesting allows more complex queries to be entered in a single statement. The following statement would be allowed if nesting is supported: (CATS OR (FELINES AND DOMESTIC) OR DOGS OR (CANINES AND DOMESTIC)) AND (FLEAS OR TICKS). The level of nesting may be limited in some systems.

Other logical operators are sometimes encountered. The XOR operator (exclusive OR) searches for terms that are in one or the other record but not in both. It is equivalent to the combination (TERM1 OR TERM2) NOT (TERM1 AND TERM2).

Set Building and Stepwise Refinement

Set building is an essential part of online retrieval systems. Pointers to the records that satisfy a given query are viewed as a set defined by that query. Set building allows a search to be performed in steps: first creating sets, then modifying them, then combining or modifying them again until the results are satisfactory. Systems supporting such stepwise refinement are more conducive to heuristic, interactive, trial-and-error searching.

The stepwise approach requires that the system be able to store (or easily regenerate) the results of each query, label these as sets (typically by assigning a sequential set number), and allow combinations of new sets with previously created ones.

In a system that does not allow the use of parentheses, the pet/pest query above might be done in steps as:

CATS OR DOGS → SET1
FLEAS OR TICKS → SET2
SET1 AND SET2 → SET3

Some systems require that each term be entered as a separate step with all logical combinations done on set numbers. With this kind of system the pet/pest search would be done in seven steps:

CATS → SET1
DOGS → SET2
FLEAS → SET3
TICKS → SET4
SET1 OR SET2 → SET5

SET3 OR SET4 → SET6
SET5 AND SET6 → SET7

Systems that support the stepwise approach frequently have a limit to the number of sets that can be accumulated. This limit is generally high enough not to be a problem.

Comparison Operators

Most fields contain values that can be ordered in some reasonable way, such as alphabetic or from greatest number to smallest. This is the basis for inverted indexes. Given some order it often makes sense to ask for records based on this ordering. Comparison operators offer a convenient means of expressing such queries. The standard set of comparison operators are $=, <, >, <=, >=$, and $<>$, which represent equal to, less than, greater than, less than or equal to, greater than or equal to, and not equal to. Some systems will use different notation such as EQ, LT, GT, LE, GE, NE.

Comparison operators are often used with numeric value fields as, for example, year of publication. A user might want to limit retrieval to recent material only and so specify YR > 1985. Or, in a file containing salary data, it would be convenient to be able to find all employees making more than (or less than) a specified amount. Similarly, it may be desirable to list all people in the file between the ages of 21 and 65. This could be done by combining relational specifications with the Boolean AND operator: AGE >= 21 AND AGE <=65.

Range Searching. Another way to search based on an ordered sequence is range searching. The words FROM and TO are frequently used to express this type of query. For example, the search on ages between 21 and 65 could be expressed as AGE FROM 21 TO 66. The inverted index aids in this type of search because the values are arranged in a range from smallest to largest. We are in effect extracting subranges from a preexisting range when we do this kind of searching.

Field Specification

Most retrieval systems allow the searcher to specify particular fields for searching, some require all searches to include a specification as to what field(s) to search, others allow default search fields to be indicated at the time the database is configured. The ability to limit a search to a particular field may speed searching and reduces false drops. WHITE? searched only on the author field, for example, will eliminate records with subject words such as whitewash, white-walls, and so on. AUTOMATION searched only as a descriptor or title word will avoid retrieving records in which the term was used just in an abstract or full text. Field specification thus allows more precision in searching.

Automatic Thesaurus

Vocabulary control provides a way to deal with problems of synonyms, homographs, and varying word forms (see Chapter 5). Most systems that use a controlled vocabulary are designed with the expectation that the user will consult a thesaurus if necessary, either in hard copy form or online. A further refinement to having a thesaurus available online is the capacity of the system to automatically look up terms in a thesaurus and substitute or expand as appropriate. For example, a searcher might enter the term U.N. and have it automatically translated to UNITED NATIONS, or MOUSE might be changed to MICE. Similarly, terms can be checked against the thesaurus in data entry, assuring quality control in those fields handled this way.

Keeping the searcher informed of the transformations that are made and giving the searcher some control over the process make it more acceptable to most users. Otherwise, problems such as automatic expansion to include plural forms may on occasion frustrate users. (For example, a search for ELECTRONIC JOURNALS might retrieve articles on ELECTRONICS JOURNALS.)

Another use of an online thesaurus is the automatic expansion of a controlled vocabulary query term to include other hierarchically related terms. For example, if under the term CANINES the thesaurus listed narrower terms DOGS, WOLVES, COYOTES, and so on, an automatic expansion feature would allow the searcher to retrieve all these terms by specifying an expansion of canines.

Unlike the other search features discussed so far, automatic thesaurus capabilities are not yet available on most retrieval systems. Among commercial online systems, Mead Data Central's LEXIS and NEXIS system, the National Library of Medicine's MEDLINE, and H. W. Wilson's WILSONLINE are notable for their vocabulary control features. Most of the software for inhouse databases on microcomputers does not support automatic thesaurus functions. It is unfortunate because such features are useful aids for better searching and quality control of input.

SPECIAL FEATURES

The search features described so far might be considered standard, and you should expect to find most of these in some form or other in a good information retrieval system (with the exception of the automatic thesaurus features). Most are facilitated by the inverted file structure discussed previously. The standard search systems based on inverted files thus provide many advantages. There are some problems, however, with the standard Boolean approach to searching. Gerard Salton (1975) lists the following:

- the difficulty in varying the search depth to retrieve a greater or lesser amount of material
- retrieval is an all or nothing process and partial matching is not accommodated. It is not possible to adjust the criteria for retrieval in terms of degree of similarity of query and documents;
- the output cannot be presented in ranked order of decreasing query-document similarity.

A number of approaches to search and retrieval have been developed in response to these problems. Many of these approaches are still experimental or are not widely used in commercial systems or inhouse database software. Only a brief mention will be made of these systems here; the Further Readings section at the end of this chapter provide sources of information on other search and retrieval methods.

Other Boolean Systems

Other approaches to the Boolean search process have been developed which do not depend on set operations with inverted files. In *weighted term query formulation* the searcher enters terms, associated weights, and a threshold weight. Document weights are then computed based on the occurrence of the terms in the documents. Those documents having a weight equal to or greater than the threshold are retrieved. For example, to search for CATS AND FLEAS the searcher could specify a weight of one for CATS and one for FLEAS with a threshold weight of two. A search for CATS OR DOGS would assign weights of one to each term and a threshold of one. While not eliminating the problems of Boolean searching systems, this approach makes it easier to formulate certain queries (e.g., any n of x terms). (See Gerrie.)

Ranked output with inverted file Boolean searching is offered by the Personal Librarian software (discussed in Chapter 7). The ranking is based on word occurrence statistics. Ranking of output in order of probable relevance also solves, in part at least, the first two problems mentioned previously, since the searcher can stop the output when the documents become less relevant. (See Noreault, Koll, and McGill.)

The *signature file* approach supports retrieval of textual data by generating a second file with a record corresponding to each record in the text file. The signatures are designed to allow rapid comparison with query signatures making sequential searching of the signature file reasonably fast.

Superimposed hashing is one method of signature file generation. It is offered in the Sci-Mate package described in Chapter 7 and in some other text retrieval software. Instead of an inverted index file, a *map file* that contains one fixed length signature or fingerprint for each record in the main file is created.

A fixed length string of ones and zeros is produced based on the particular combination of short character sequences in the records and in the query terms. *Hashing* is the term used to describe the mathematical transformation of the character sequence into a number that will point to a particular bit in the signature string that is set to one. (Those not pointed to in the hashing process remain zeros.) Searching involves the comparison of the query signature against each record signature, retrieving those records having ones in each position where ones occur in the query signature. (See Faloutsos.)

There is a chance for a small percentage of false drops with this method, so in some systems the records retrieved are then searched by the standard string searching method. Since the retrieved set is generally a small subset of the entire file, this usually does not take long.

Fuzzy Sets

In the usual approach to assigning subject descriptors, the indexer decides whether or not a term is applicable to a document. In reality, however, index terms describe particular documents more or less well. The fuzzy set approach allows for the indication of the degree to which a term fits a document. This is indicated by assigning a weight of between zero and one to each term. The retrieval process is similar to normal Boolean retrieval except that output can be ranked and a cutoff weight can be specified and adjusted interactively. As an example of fuzzy logic, we might have a document with term A assigned a weight of 0.7 and term B a weight of 0.3. Fuzzy A AND B would yield a weight of 0.3 (the minimum of the two term weights) and fuzzy A OR B would yield a weight of 0.7 (the maximum of the two weights). A user could specify that only documents with a certain weight or greater would be retrieved.

Cluster Files and Similarity Measures

The calculation of a similarity coefficient for each pair of records in a file can provide a basis for retrieval. This approach has been studied at length by Gerard Salton and coworkers with the SMART system. Essentially, records are grouped or clustered according to their similarity to one another, based on word occurrence data.

Queries are expressed in natural language and are processed in the same way as were the records in the database. Those records that are most similar to the query are retrieved. This approach can also be used with a known record as a query. The system will find others similar to it based on word occurrence data. The Personal Librarian software described in Chapter 7 includes such a *like document* search feature.

Relevance Feedback

The typical set building and stepwise refinement approach to searching offers the searcher the possibility of examining intermediate results and modifying the search strategy accordingly. Some systems display intermediate results, ask the searcher to indicate which records are relevant and which are not, then automatically modify the query to increase the retrieval of records similar to those designated as relevant while decreasing the retrieval of records similar to the nonrelevant records found in the earlier trial. Some of the systems described previously make use of this approach, changing the weighting of terms to favor those occurring in the relevant records more frequently than in nonrelevant ones.

THE USER-SYSTEM INTERFACE

An area that has often been neglected in information storage and retrieval software design is the interface between the user and the software. The user-system interface will often determine whether people use a database or not. A program that is capable of doing all that needs to be done may not be used if the users find it too difficult or intimidating. Software that meets these user-system interface concerns is termed "user-friendly."

Acceptable interactive software, at the very least, must produce the desired results, must be adequately documented, and must provide sufficient control so that the user can produce the desired outcome. Beyond this, more is required to make the experience pleasant or at least to minimize the user's frustration.

Requirements for user friendliness might be divided into two categories: (1) protecting the users from themselves (sometimes referred to as idiot proofing), and (2) facilitating program use.

Idiot Proofing

Users of software will invariably make mistakes even when the software is easy to learn. When the mistakes are handled in a positive helpful manner, users will gain confidence in the system and feel less intimidated or fearful of damaging the system or the data.

Specific features to look for in protecting the user include the following. The software should:

- shield the user from system failures (backup facilities will help here, within and external to the program);
- cope with user errors, such as incorrect responses, pressing control keys, not responding at all;
- allow the user to undo past system action, to cancel the result of an erroneous command or menu choice;
- warn the user if irrevocable action (such as file deletion) is asked for.

Facilitating Program Use

Beyond having a program that will produce the desired results with the correct input and that will cope with any invalid input, there are several features that can facilitate effective use:

- Documentation, in the form of clear and complete user manuals.
- Online help, including clear and explicit error messages in terms the user can understand and a HELP command offering context-sensitive help, preferably with several levels, depending on the user's needs.

- An easy to learn, user-oriented system language. Terminology used in menus or a command language should be readily understandable to the users. The application should provide the semantic constraints necessary. Users should be able to express the same thing in more than one way. Natural language systems must be capable of dealing with the user's vocabulary and syntax.
- Multiple levels of interaction to accommodate users with varying levels of experience. At least two levels, a short mode for experienced users and a normal mode for beginners, should be provided. As many as four levels might be offered: tutorial, menu driven, prompting, and command driven.
- The ability to interrupt work with the software and come back later to pick up where the user left off.
- Orderly, uncluttered, easy-to-read screen displays. Effective use of color and/or other video effects such as reverse video, underlining, and so on.
- Consistent terminology, commands, formats, and general appearance among the various modules. As much as possible what is learned in one module should transfer to others.

FURTHER READINGS

Belkin, Nicholas J. and Vickery, Alina. *Interaction in Information Systems: A Review of Research From Document Retrieval to Knowledge-Based Systems*. Boston Spa: British Library Lending Division, 1985.

Belkin, Nicholas; Croft, W. Bruce. "Retrieval Techniques." *Annual Review of Information Science and Technology*. 20 (1987): 109–145.

Bookstein, Abraham. "Probability and Fuzzy-Set Applications to Information Retrieval." *Annual Review of Information Science and Technology* 20 (1985): 117–151.

Colvin, Gregory. "Database Retrieval and Indexing." In *CD ROM: Volume 2, Optical Publishing*. 103–117. Edited by Suzanne Ropiequet. Redmond, WA: Microsoft Press, 1987.

Faloutsos, C. "Access Methods for Text." *ACM Computing Surveys* 17 (March 1985): 49–74.

Fand, Jerry. "Full Text Retrieval and Indexing." In *CD ROM: Volume 2, Optical Publishing*. 83–102. Edited by Suzanne Ropiequet. Redmond, WA: Microsoft Press, 1987.

Fox, Edward A. "Information Retrieval: Research Into New Capabilities." In *CD/ROM: The New Papyrus*. 143–174. Edited by Steve Lambert and Suzanne Ropiequet. Redmond, Wash.: Microsoft Press, 1986.

Gerrie, Brenda. *Online Information Systems: Use and Operating Character-istics, Limitations, and Design Alternatives.* Arlington, Va.: Information Resources Press, 1983.

Humphrey, Susanne M. and Melloni, Biagio John. *Databases: A Primer for Retrieving Information by Computer.* Englewood Cliffs, N.J.: Prentice-Hall, 1986.

Noreault, T.; McGill, Michael J.; and Koll, Matthew B. "A Performance Evaluation of Similarity Measures, Document Term Weighting Schemes and Representation in a Boolean Environment." In *Information Retrieval Research.* 57–76. Edited by R.N. Oddy, S.E. Robertson, C.J. Van Rijsbergen, and P.W. Williams. London: Butterworths, 1981.

Rowley, J.E. "Text Retrieval Systems—An Outline." *Oxford Surveys in Information Technology* 3 (1986): 211–245.

Salton, Gerard. *Dynamic Information and Library Processing.* Englewood Cliffs, N.J.: Prentice-Hall, 1975.

Salton, Gerard and McGill, Michael J. *Introduction to Modern Information Retrieval.* New York: McGraw-Hill, 1983.

Tenopir, Carol. "Data Base Design and Management." In *The Theory and Practice of Information Science.* Edited by John Olsgaard. Chicago: ALA, 1988. In press.

Wallace, Danny P. "A Preliminary Examination of the Meaning of User Friendliness." In *Proceedings of the 48th American Society for Information Science Annual Meeting,* 337–341. White Plains, N.Y.: Knowledge Industry Publications, 1985.

Williams, Martha E., et al. "Comparative Analysis of Online Retrieval Interfaces." In *Proceedings of the 49th American Society for Information Science Annual Meeting,* 365–370. Medford, N.J.: Learned Information, 1986.

Zoellick, Bill. "Selecting an Approach to Document Retrieval." In *CD ROM: Volume 2, Optical Publishing.* 63–82. Edited by Suzanne Ropiequet. Redmond, WA: Microsoft Press, 1987.

4
Feasibility Study

Designers of inhouse databases often want to immediately choose the hardware and software for their project and get quickly to the stage of inputting records. Those are certainly the steps that are the most rewarding in terms of seeing a real product, but they are prone to frustration, delay, and sometimes even failure if the proper groundwork is not laid first.

This early process may be called the "preliminary needs analysis," "needs assessment," "preliminary specifications," "systems analysis," or "feasibility study." In reality, it includes all of these and could more precisely be defined as the preliminary planning process. Throughout *Managing Your Information* feasibility study refers to the process of creating a written planning document encompassing all the steps described in this chapter. In a large organization or for a very large database, the process may be used to create a specifications document to be used in a formal bidding process by software vendors. For most inhouse databases, however, the feasibility study will be carried out by you, the database designer, perhaps with the help of a database committee. Especially for microcomputer-based systems, it may never be seen by anyone else.

Regardless of the size of your project or eventual distribution of your feasibility study, a thorough definition of the scope of your project and a written analysis of the needs of the potential users of the database are crucial first steps. They may take longer than the later actual creation stages, but are well worth the time and effort involved to ensure creation of a database that accomplishes what you want it to do.

The purpose of the feasibility study is to focus on the information to be included in the database and on the users of the database. This will allow you to first determine if an inhouse database is even appropriate and, if so, to identify the factors that will affect all of the steps of the database design. The purpose of any database, whether it has 500 records or 50,000 records, should be to provide improved access to information for users—preferably in a more efficient and effective manner. To do so, the database design-er must have a thorough understanding of the characteristics of the information to be included in the database, of the use patterns and retrieval needs of the potential users, and how these factors interrelate. Whether you are converting an existing manual system, such as a card catalog, or designing a database from scratch, it is essential that you first go through the preliminary feasibility study steps.

THE DATABASE COMMITTEE

If your database will be used by large numbers of people in an organization, you may wish to form a database committee to help with the feasibility study process. The committee serves to get many different people at all levels involved from the outset. This will not only allow you to divide the database design tasks, it will help to ensure that your design reflects the needs of all types of users. It will also focus attention in your organization on the database project. The final database will, therefore, be more likely to be used if it is designed with all users in mind and if it has gotten exposure from the beginning. In addition, an organization-wide committee will be able to focus on database needs beyond the current project. This wider focus may be important in the software evaluation process if a package is to be selected that best meets all database needs within the organization.

The database committee can be composed of between three and 12 people, including representatives from the following groups:

- end users (from various departments)
- intermediary users
- clerical inputters
- representatives from the data processing or information manage-ment department
- management (those who have control over expenditures)

The representatives should be involved from the beginning of the process if possible. They should have tasks assigned that make the best use of their unique interests and talents at every step in the database design process. There must always be one person in charge, however, who can make assignments and final decisions. That person will most likely be you, the database designer.

PURPOSES OF THE FEASIBILITY STUDY

Whether there is an existing manual retrieval system of some sort that will be converted or a database system will be created from scratch, the purposes of the feasibility study are similar. These purposes are to

- describe the current collection and any current access to it
- identify current and potential users of the system
- discover the main purpose and importance of the collection
- identify important information flows in the existing system (e.g., how do people use a card file to find information; how is the card file updated)
- isolate problems with current use
- discover possible solutions to each problem
- estimate the dollar and time resources necessary for the project
- identify potential benefits of the new system
- uncover budget, hardware, software, and personnel constraints
- begin the database design process
- assess the impact of the new system on the users and physical environment
- set the framework for the proposed software evaluation process
- eliminate over-expectation and under-delivery of the overall system capabilities
- identify needed capabilities and necessary design features

If there is no existing manual system, the focus of the feasibility study will be on the nature of the materials to be included in the database, the potential users, and the hoped for capabilities and uses of the new system.

Figure 4.1 is a sample table of contents for a preliminary feasibility study for an inhouse database. Although the feasibility study is primarily a *process,* the *product* will be a draft document that summarizes all of the information gathered. This document need not necessarily be lengthy or elaborate, but by creating it in a structured, written form it will be useful throughout the subsequent design and creation steps. Appendix A includes the preliminary feasibility study for an inhouse database that was designed by a library consultant for a group of doctors.

The feasibility study will evolve and change as the project progresses, so the goal is not to create a polished, final document at this early stage. Every bit of information that is gathered in the preliminary feasibility study and is listed in Figure 4.1 will be useful later to design field structures, evaluate software, or make other design decisions.

There are two main sections to the preliminary feasibility study: the present situation and the desired system. The second part will change the most throughout the design process. For both of these you will be concentrating on discovering three categories of information: the needs and desires of the eventual end users of the database; the needs and desires of the people responsible for maintaining the collection and the database; and the characteristics of the collection and of the information going into the database. Although stated differently, these three categories of requirements are all built into the information gathering process outlined in Figure 4.1.

THE PRESENT SITUATION

Assessing the present situation in terms of the requirements above is primarily a data gathering and descriptive process. Since access to a collection of information is the reason for creating an inhouse database, it is important to first identify and describe this collection.

Describe the Collection

Assume, for instance, that a collection of textual materials exists that will eventually make up your database. The existence of such a collection and the desire to provide better access to it is probably the motivation for creating an inhouse database in the first place. The physical texts or documents in this collection may ultimately either be described in a bibliographic database or the documents as a whole may be included in a full text database or a directory database. At this preliminary stage you might not know for sure which option is desirable or feasible. The collection may or may not be accessible currently through some sort of retrieval system, such as a card catalog. Both the collection and the retrieval system (if any) need to be described. (If no collection yet exists, see Chapter 5.)

The existing collection should first be described in terms of document characteristics and collection size. This will affect many decisions, notably the choice between a bibliographic or full text database and hardware and software choice, and it will give you a

FIGURE 4.1   Table of Contents for a Preliminary Feasibility Study

I. The present situation
   A. Describe the collection
      1. Types of items
         a. characteristics (age, length, languages, physical description, etc.)
         b. subjects
      2. Number of items
      3. Characteristics of specific item elements (e.g., length of titles, number of authors, abstracts or summaries present, etc.)
      4. Where it is kept, physical description, space limitations
      5. Why the collection is important
   B. Describe current access system and use of collection
      1. Access points if any
      2. Who maintains collection and how often
      3. Who maintains access system and how often
      4. Who uses collection or access system and how often
      5. Records in machine-readable form
   C. Why a new system is needed
      1. Problems with current system
      2. Advantages of current system
   D. Hardware, software, and personnel situation
      1. Is there hardware now inhouse?
         a. Describe (brand, model, size of internal memory, external storage capacity, operating systems)
         b. How much used
         c. Will it be replaced in future
         d. Priority of this database
         e. Must it be used
      2. May you purchase hardware
         a. Must it be used for other things
         b. Reasonable price range
         c. Restrictions on brand or model
      3. Is there database, file management, or information retrieval software inhouse
         a. What software (type, name, producer)
         b. Is it being used inhouse
         c. Do you know anyone using it for textual databases
      4. May you purchase software
         a. Must it be used for other applications
         b. Reasonable price range
         c. Restrictions on supplier
      5. Are there programmers inhouse
         a. Priority of this application
         b. What programming languages are supported
         c. Experience with textual databases

II. The desired system
  A. Users
    1. Who will users be
      a. Different levels and expertise
      b. Number of users and how many at once
      c. Will an intermediary be present
      d. Anticipated amount of use
      e. Where will system be accessed
    2. Who will maintain system and collection
  B. Access
    1. What access points are needed
    2. How much information should be in the database
      a. Full text (does it all need to be searchable)
      b. Should abstracts be included (searchable)
    3. Desired searching features (e.g., Boolean combinations, calculations, sorting, etc.)
    4. Prioritize features
    5. Output requirements
  C. Database future
    1. Expected number of records in database now
    2. How much will it grow, and how fast will it grow
      a. Weeding
      b. Additions
    3. Updates
    4. Likely editorial changes (how much of database will be affected)
    5. What will system look like in one year, five years, ten years.

---

head start in writing your database documentation. The following points should be described:

1. What types of materials are in the collection? Are they textual materials, such as journal articles, research reports, books, names and addresses, or a combination of textual types? Are they non-textual physical objects such as software, photographs, architectural or engineering drawings, maps, realia, or a combination?
2. If the collection consists of written materials, what are the maximum, minimum, and average lengths of the documents? If the collection consists of physical objects, what are their important characteristics?
3. For documents, what languages are they written in? Will translation of the entire documents or bibliographic information be necessary? Will records in the database be wholly or partly in their original languages? If the latter is a possibility, make special note of non-Roman languages, the need for special characters, and diacritics.

4. What are the main subjects of the collection? Are main subjects distinguishable or is the collection a combination of many subjects? (This may impact your later decisions regarding choice of controlled vocabulary indexing.)
5. What is the current size of the collection (i.e., the total number of documents that will be included in the database)?

All of the above descriptions apply as well with some modifications to collections of items such as software, photographs, or realia. These types of collections will not, of course, be considered for a full text database; instead a bibliographic-type description will point to the location of the physical object. Fully describe the physical characteristics of the collection no matter what it contains. For a microcomputer software collection, the description may include the size and format of the disks; the maximum, minimum, and average number of programs on each disk; accompanying documentation, if any; the different subjects included in the collection; the hardware requirements to run the disks; programming languages; and the total number of disks as well as the total number of programs.

In addition to describing the characteristics of the collection as a whole, you should begin to describe the characteristics of the individual data elements of items. A reprint collection, for example, may consist of several thousand journal article reprints. Reprints typically have titles that may vary from five to 200 characters. Estimate the shortest, longest, and average. The reprints may also typically have between zero and ten personal authors, a single journal title, and citation information. Most may have author-written abstracts at the beginning of the article or summaries at the end. By describing the characteristics of typical and exceptional documents in the collection at this early design stage, later you will be able to more easily make decisions about the content of your database and design your record structure as described in Chapter 6.

Once you have completed the analysis of the characteristics of the materials in the collection, you should describe where the collection is now kept and under what conditions. The physical surroundings, including space limitations, may be justification for creating a full text database or may, at least, provide incentive for weeding before the database is created.

Finally in your description of the collection, include a statement of why the collection is important and to whom it is important. If the collection is not of importance, why go to the trouble and expense of creating a database to provide access to it?

Describe Current Access and Use

Once the collection itself is described, the feasibility study should focus on the current process for accessing the collection. This section may be very simple—there may as yet be no way to access the materials in the collection. At the other extreme, there may be an elaborate manual, or even an outdated automated, retrieval system that provides access to the materials in the collection. Most common are simple author or date physical filing systems or more elaborate subject indexing systems.

No matter how simple or complex the existing access system, the database designer must describe it in sufficient detail to discover the current and potential use, how it is maintained, and its strengths and weaknesses. Describe:

1. What are the current access points if any (e.g., filed by author or date, indexed by subjects)?
2. Who is responsible for maintaining the system, the jobs involved in this maintenance (e.g., cataloging, preparing cards, filing, and so on), and how many hours per week or per month are spent on the maintenance? (In many instances the system maintainer and database designer will be the same person. This does not eliminate the need for this description, it just makes it easier.)
3. Who uses the system? (You will be interviewing users in the later stages of the feasibility study, so try to find out names of specific users as well as categories of users.)
4. Are any records now in machine readable form? If there are, describe their format in detail and include an example. (If you are describing an automated system that will be converted in whole or in part to a new system, the old system will need to be described in detail.)

Why a New System Is Needed

The collection and system descriptions discussed so far require a close examination of what presently exists. In a sense, the entire purpose of this first part of the preliminary feasibility study is to discover if a new system is needed, to articulate why, and to justify its creation by discussing the advantages and disadvantages of the present system with the current users and system maintainers. Your examination so far may have revealed some obvious problems. Inadequate access points, time-consuming maintenance procedures, or the lack of any retrieval system may all be problems that surface in the early data gathering phases. At this point, a short narrative description of these problems and why they make the new database system desirable provides a useful summary that can be elaborated on later if further justification is needed.

Hardware/Software Situation

Once you have described the collection, its current access and use, and summarized your findings of why a new system is needed, the data gathering stage concludes with a description of the present hardware, software, and personnel situation. This is important in order to identify potential constraints of budget, time, and other resources and to lay the groundwork for the important decision process concerning hardware and software.

Information that should be gathered includes: *A short description of any computers* that are now in your organization that may potentially be used for your database. You need not be a computer expert to list the brand name and model, the operating systems supported, and how much the computer is currently being used. The amount of use should be recorded both in terms of number of hours used per day and in percent of disk capacity in use. Also, if possible, find out from management what priority your database application will have. Try to find out from your data processing manager or the person in charge if there are plans to replace this equipment in the near future or if upgrades or additional equipment are forthcoming. Find out if the inhouse computer *must* be used (or on the other hand, if it cannot be used) for your database.

Can you purchase hardware? If so, must it be shared with other departments or used for other applications in addition to your database? Are there limitations on the price you will be able to pay, or is there a company policy that places limitations on the brand or model purchased? Some organizations are now formulating policies that restrict microcomputer purchases to one brand throughout the company. If your company will only allow you to buy an IBM-PC, for example, find this out now! It may not be a problem, but it will limit your software options.

Are there programmers inhouse to assist you? If there are, find out what programming languages they support and what experience, if any, they have with textual databases. This could have an impact on your software choice. Find out from management what priority your database application will have in terms of staff programming time.

Are there programs already inhouse that may be suitable? At this stage, merely identify the programs by name and begin to read about them. Any program already inhouse should be evaluated as carefully as a new program to be purchased. Do not automatically assume an existing program will meet your database needs.

Can you purchase software and with what monetary constraints? It is important to realize general constraints at an early stage, but avoid setting a hard and fast dollar limit at this point if at all possible. Additionally, find out from management or the data processing staff if there are any limitations on the sources you will be allowed to use to purchase software.

THE DESIRED SYSTEM

The example of a feasibility study in Appendix A illustrates that the first part of the preliminary feasibility study need not be lengthy. As a first step, it must be detailed enough to set the groundwork for your later decision-making processes as well as perhaps forming the beginning of a justification document for creation of a database. The second part of the preliminary feasibility study actually begins the design process and will take more time.

Part two of the feasibility study, The Desired System, may undergo several drafts and will surely be revised several times as you continue the design process described in subsequent chapters of *Managing Your Information*. It is a working document, a necessary step before you can proceed logically through the design and creation process. The information to be included in this section is described first, followed by some hints on how to gather the information.

The desired system can be described in three categories—users, access needed, and the future of the database. In all three cases, you may only be guessing or predicting at this point, but this early description will provide the framework for all other decisions.

Users

Try to identify all potential users of the database or categories of users as specifically as possible. In a small research and development department this may be easy. You may know all of the individuals who will benefit from the database. In a public library situation, on the other hand, you may only have a notion of the types of people who will eventually use the database. In either case, however, be as specific as possible. This will help you later in your database design, user interface design, software choice, and the writing of the database documentation.

Potential users and usage should be described in terms of:

1. Who will the users be? Do they have experience with information retrieval systems or do they now use other databases? Are there several categories or classes of users, some with database experience and some without? What are their educational levels and their motivation for getting information from the database? These will have important ramifications in your software choice and in the design of your user-software interface.
2. How many total users are expected and how many would be likely to use the database at the same time? This will directly affect your choice of hardware and software.
3. Will an intermediary or someone familiar with the database be present when people are using it? If users must learn to use the system alone and solve their own problems, the software will need to include more user-friendly features and clear error messages.
4. Try to anticipate the amount of use. Will the system be used all day or will there be peak and lag periods? The hardware used for the database may be able to be used for other things if there will be long stretches of low database use.
5. Related to points three and four is the question of where the system will be accessed. Will it be accessed only in a central location (as in a library), or will users need access from their offices or homes? Is access desirable from several central locations? This will greatly affect your hardware and software selection.

In addition to focusing on the end users of the database, it is important to begin to identify maintenance personnel. If there is an experienced staff of librarians with clerical assistants ready to keep the database up-to-date, design decisions can reflect this. If a part-time secretary is to be solely responsible for upkeep and maintenance, it is best to know this at the beginning, so a simple-to-maintain system can be designed. Any database must be designed with *all* users and *all* levels of personnel constantly in mind.

Access

Probably the most important part of the preliminary feasibility study, and the one that leads most directly to the design stage and software evaluation, is the section on access. This information will also undergo the most revisions as the design process progresses, especially if your experience with databases is limited. Beginning to gather this information is a crucial step in the design and creation process, and one that will involve interaction with potential system users and maintainers. Do not get discouraged easily at this stage— often the database designer and future users learn together as the project evolves.

The most important thing to remember early on is to dream with users about access under the ideal circumstances. You are not promising yet what the system will look like, but you do want to discover what users would really like in an ideal system. Later, compromises may need to be made, but you may be surprised at how much of what you consider ideal is possible with today's microcomputer-based information retrieval software.

An overview of interviewing tactics is given at the conclusion of this chapter. In interviews with users you will be attempting to determine a variety of information. For instance, *What access points are needed?* In the ideal situation, how would each user search for information in the database? Would they like to be able to find materials by subjects, by date of publication, by authors? Would it be useful to find an article by its title? Would there ever be a need to get a list of all books published by a certain publisher or in a particular language? The key to finding this information is to get users to dream about all the access possibilities without worrying about perceived constraints. (Librarians will recognize this as good reference interview technique.) (The compilation of all desired access points will lead directly to the field definition stage described in Chapter 6.)

How much information should be in the database? If it is to be a bibliographic database, are abstracts or annotations necessary? In a referral database, is descriptive information desirable in addition to names and addresses? Is full text important or essential?

What searching features are needed? If numeric information is included in the database, will mathematical calculations be necessary or desirable? Will users want to combine search terms (finding all articles on a certain subject written in a specified year, for example), necessitating Boolean logic combinations? Would it be useful to sort output by some criteria, such as alphabetical by author?

Once all desirable search features have been identified, you should set priorities for them. Which features are essential immediately, which are not needed at present but will be essential in the future, and which are desirable but not required?

After searching features have been identified and prioritized, output requirements can be stated. Will the users primarily be using the database online to find information on a CRT screen, or would a customized printout of search results also be useful? Are printouts of the entire database needed, as an author/title/subject catalog for example? The output capabilities of software vary greatly, so it is essential to anticipate as many desirable types of output as possible.

Database Future

The final section of the feasibility study should address future requirements and directions. Much of this may depend on how the database is initially received by users, but anticipating future directions now will help ensure positive reception and to circumvent later problems.

Address the following points:

1. What is the total expected size of the database, including all of the present collection? This will be stated in number of records for now (e.g., 5,000 articles in the collection equals 5,000 records in the database). As the design progresses it will be stated in terms of numbers of characters.
2. How much and at what rate will the database grow? This can be estimated by anticipating the number of items to be added to a collection each month or each year, minus the number to be deleted or weeded.
3. How often will the database need to be updated? Will this change in the near future?
4. Do you anticipate making wholesale editorial changes to the database in the future? For example, will you be updating outmoded subject descriptors.
5. How do you, the users, and the maintainers of the collection envision this database at the end of one year, five years, and even ten years? Will it be the first module in an organization-wide series of databases? Will it provide bibliographic access for the present, but eventually include the full texts of materials? Will it be available only in your organization now, but eventually be commercially available?

This future vision will help to summarize why this database is important and how it will evolve in the near future. It will help you make wise decisions that will save frustration in the future.

MANUAL VS. AUTOMATED

One decision that may be made during or immediately after the feasibility study is the decision that a database is not desirable in your situation. As in any automation project, automating an unneeded collection or an ill-conceived project may only increase costs or complicate problems. If the feasibility study shows that the collection is important and that access is needed, a manual system may still be the better solution in some cases.

A manual system *may* be best if the feasibility study reveals a majority of the following characteristics:

- the collection is static (no new items will be added nor old items weeded)
- the information is static (records will never be updated or corrected)
- limited access points are needed
- access is needed in only one location
- hardware maintenance is a problem (for example, in a remote location)
- current hardware or software is badly outdated or inadequate, and new equipment cannot be purchased
- the collection is very small, and the cost of purchasing hardware and software must be justified for this project alone
- a current manual system works fine, and users are happy with it
- conversion costs will be prohibitive, and you have no funds or personnel to do the conversion adequately
- you do not have the time to do a proper job of system design
- you do not have the time to do a proper job of system documentation and user training
- there is no commitment to the project from management or users.

The existence of only one or two of these conditions (except perhaps the last) need not be fatal for your project, but if your preliminary feasibility study reveals several of these conditions, the wisest course may be to develop a manual system or stick with the current system. Be wary of arbitrary cut-offs for databases based only on number of records. There is no magic cut-off point below which an automated file cannot be successful or cost effective. Even databases of a few hundred records can be economical and beneficial on a microcomputer-based system.

The decision to automate should be based on many factors, not just sheer number of documents in a collection. Record size, access points needed, update schedules, and so on all affect the decision to create a database. With the low cost of today's hardware and some software, it is becoming more difficult to justify new manual systems for even small collections.

COST-BENEFIT ANALYSIS

A full cost-benefit analysis is rarely undertaken except for the largest inhouse database. Still, you may be called upon to justify your decision to create a database and may need to demonstrate that the benefits outweigh the probable costs. A complete discussion of cost-benefit techniques are beyond the scope of this book, but readers are referred to the practical advice in articles and books by John King and Edward Schrems, N.M.S. Cox and C.K. Balmforth, and R.I. Benjamin.

If, after your preliminary feasibility study is completed, you doubt the advisability of continuing the database project further, or if you find you must justify it to management, you will need to weigh the probable benefits against the probable costs. Both anticipated tangible and intangible benefits should be listed first. These will include such things as lower maintenance costs as well as such things as increased access to information. Many of these benefits will be obvious from your feasibility study. General benefits that may be realized by having an inhouse database include increased access points to the collection, speedier retrieval of information, ability to perform complex combinations of search terms, generation of customized reports, the ability to make multiple copies of the file, capability of accessing system from multiple locations, speedier updating and corrections, the ability to make changes easily in the data, and lower maintenance costs.

To weigh benefits against costs, you must of course identify all possible costs associated with the planned database. These costs will include personnel costs to continue the design and creation stages, maintenance costs once the database is designed, and all hardware and software costs. After the preliminary feasibility study is completed, you will have some of the information necessary to calculate personnel and maintenance costs, but you will not yet have enough information for exact hardware and software costs. You will thus need to begin the software investigation process described in Chapter 8 to obtain full anticipated costs. Possible costs associated with inhouse databases include personnel costs to do a systems analysis and for the database design process, software purchase and upgrade price, hardware purchase or upgrade price, increased computer storage capacity (e.g., purchase a hard disk), data conversion costs, ongoing input costs, editing and revising costs, hardware maintenance, cost to make copies of the database for distribution, documentation creation costs, and costs to train users.

GATHERING INFORMATION

Several techniques may be used to gather the information you need to complete the preliminary feasibility study. To get the information you need to answer all of the sections in the feasibility study, you should:

- conduct interviews
- examine documents in the collection
- examine any existing manuals or documentation
- observe use of the existing system
- test usage of the existing system
- reverify all information with the primary user

A combination of these techniques should be used, but the first (interviews) is probably the most important. At the beginning of your project you should identify and interview the person or persons who have the major responsibility for the collection, the person or persons (if any) responsible for maintaining the current retrieval system, current users of the collection, and potential users once the database is in place.

Figure 4.1 can be used as an aid to develop an informal interview schedule. Much of the information in Part Two (the desired system) will come from these interviews. If you are working with a database committee, representatives from each of these groups should be members of the committee.

Questionnaires are sometimes used in place of a personal interview if there are many users or potential users of the system. A questionnaire, however, has several disadvantages. You cannot explain the purpose of the database in terms each individual will find meaningful, nor educate potential users about what an automated retrieval system can do that a manual one cannot, nor clear up any ambiguities that may be in your questions. For these reasons, personal interviews of users are recommended for most inhouse database situations.

Much of the factual information in Part One of the feasibility study is best compiled by examining the physical collection and any existing system that provides data for it. Every item in a collection does not need to be examined, measured, and described, but you should try to examine a representative sample of items. For a reprint collection stored in file cabinets, for example, you might randomly select file drawers and then documents within these drawers. You will identify and record characteristics of these documents, including extremes (e.g., longest or shortest documents), unusual documents, and average documents.

If there is a current retrieval system, you should make copies of sample records, note access points and usage patterns, and describe how the system is maintained. Remember, that simple filing order is a form of retrieval system, so note how items are physically arranged. Other manuals or user aids such as a thesaurus, cataloging instructions, or tutorials should also be identified.

A good way to determine if an existing system is working is to observe people using it. If level of use warrants observation, station yourself near the physical collection (or near any existing retrieval tools) and watch people using it. When they are ready to leave, ask them to describe to you what they were looking for, how they were looking, and whether or not they were successful in their search. They might have suggestions about retrieval points that would have made an unsuccessful search better.

Testing usage is another way to determine the successes and failures of an existing retrieval system. Devise sample queries and look for information yourself. Did you find useful information? How long did it take? Would it have been easier to find something if you had been able to use other access points? Although somewhat artificial, testing may suggest ways to design your database.

Finally, all information gathered by the above methods should be verified with the person or persons who are responsible for the collection and its use. They will not only be able to clear up any misconceptions in your feasibility study, but seeing the consolidated information may suggest further requirements of the future system to them. The best inhouse database retrieval systems reflect the unique information needs of the people for whom they are designed.

FURTHER READING

Benjamin, R. I. *Control of the Information System Development Cycle.* New York: Wiley-Interscience, 1971.

Couger, Daniel. *The Benefit Side of Cost/Benefit Analysis.* Philadelphia: Auerbach, 1975.

Cox, N.S.M. and Balmforth, C.K. "Some Notes on Costs and Benefits." In *Interface: Library Automation with Special Reference to Computing Activity.* Cambridge, Mass.: MIT Press, 1971. Reprinted in: Matthews, Joseph R. *A Reader on Choosing an Automated Library System.* Chicago, Ill.: American Library Association, 1983. 91–98.

Ercegovac, Zorana. "Evaluation and Selection of Commercial Software Systems." In *Proceedings of the 4th National Online Meeting,* 127–137. Medford, N.J.: Learned Information, 1983.

King, John Leslie and Schrems, Edward L. "Cost-Benefit Analysis in Information Systems Development and Operation." *Computing Surveys* (March 1978). Reprinted in: Matthews, Joseph R. *A Reader on Choosing an Automated Library System.* Chicago, Ill.: American Library Association, 1983. 70–90.

Matthews, Joseph R. "Needs Analysis," chapter 2 in: *Choosing an Automated Library System,* 10–25. Chicago: American Library Association, 1980.

Tenopir, Carol. "Evaluation of Library Retrieval Software." In *Communicating Information: Proceedings of the 43rd Annual Meeting of the American Society for Information Science,* vol. 17, 64–67. White Plains, N.Y.: Knowledge Industry Publications, 1980.

Tenopir, Carol. "Software for In-House Databases: Part II, Evaluation and Choice." *Library Journal* 108 (May 1, 1983): 88–89.

Tenopir, Carol. "Identification and Evaluation of Software for Microcomputer-Based In-House Databases." *Information Technology and Libraries* 3 (March 1984): 21–34.

5

Initial Editorial Decisions and Value-Added Fields

Certain decisions about the scope and content of the database must be made at the beginning of the design process. Other editorial decisions will be made later as the database takes form. These editorial steps can be separated into three types: content, structural, and procedural.

Content decisions are made before the database is created and are covered in this chapter. *Structural* decisions begin after the feasibility study and continue to be refined throughout the subsequent design and creation process. They are introduced in this chapter but are discussed in more detail in Chapter 6. *Procedural* editorial decisions are policies established to ensure the ongoing maintenance of the newly created database and are discussed in Chapter 9.

CONTENT DECISIONS

Content decisions are those editorial decisions that define the scope of both the collection and the database that provides access to it. (In a full text or referral database they may be the same thing.) Content decisions are made before a database is created, either as a result of the scrutiny that results from the preliminary feasibility study or before the feasibility study is done. Many content decisions reflect what is in the collection itself and must therefore be undertaken whether or not an automated system is created. Conscious, documented content decisions (like collection development policies in libraries) help all of the users of a collection and its retrieval system to know what they can expect to find or not find through a database.

Initial content decisions include decisions about: information included, extent of coverage, editions, country of origin, language, and full text vs. bibliographic.

Information Included

Most inhouse databases are fairly narrow in scope and include easily recognized subject or content boundaries. Your feasibility study will have identified the purpose and subjects in the collection. Definition of the items covered in a collection and subsequently in the database may or may not be within the province of the database designer. Still, the designer should be responsible for reviewing previous decisions so that the full scope of the database is clearly understood. The scope will affect field specification, software evaluation, and documentation.

It is one thing to decide that all information about tropical agriculture, for example, will be in the system and another to define and locate *all* such data. Does *all* mean all of the published literature about tropical agriculture, or all of the journal articles, or all things readily available in the United States? Does *all* include conference proceedings, names and addresses of knowledgeable people in the field, and government documents produced by third-world nations?

The definition of the scope obviously has a major impact on the users of your system. Your content decisions will limit what information is available—something that may be either negative or positive. Limiting by clearly defined criteria can reduce an overwhelming amount of material to a manageable size or serve as a quality filter. On the other hand, you may be restricting people's access to information, sometimes based only on convenience. As long as your decisions on scope are conscious and well documented, however, at least users will know the limitations and strengths of your retrieval system.

Many bibliographic or full text database producers choose to limit the scope of their database to journal articles. They select journals that are the most well-known or most widely available on a subject and publish a list of titles of the journals covered in their database. This provides an easily understood definition of scope and also allows for periodic additions or changes in the scope.

A bibliographic database that is a description of a library's collection sometimes has an easily defined scope of every book or journal owned by that library, or every book or journal purchased since a certain date.

Decisions on the information to be included in a collection or a database will affect the cost of gathering items, the time and cost of preparing them for input, and the size of your database. As with any decision, you must balance the time and costs involved with the needs

FIGURE 5.1   Information Included in the Tuna Fish Database

The Tuna Fish database attempts to collect and index worldwide research based information about any species of tuna fish. The source publications indexed in the database include professional journals, unpublished research reports, monographs, and dissertations. Excluded from the database are popular magazine articles, newspaper stories, and secondary reports of research if the primary source is available.

Any research based publication that discusses such things as the breeding, habits, diseases, or behavior of tuna fish will be included. Excluded is anything about government fishing policies.

An attempt is made to obtain a copy of each item indexed to be kept in the departmental offices, but even items not readily available will be included in the database if enough descriptive information is known.

of the users. Since you have a clear idea of your user's needs from the preliminary feasibility study, this part of the project should be easier. Figure 5.1 is an example of a policy on information included for an inhouse bibliographic database.

Extent of Coverage

The next level of detail in content decisions is the extent of coverage of the items described or included in the database. It is not enough to define the scope as the books that are housed in a particular library. You must decide, for example, whether access will be only to each book as a whole or to every chapter in a book. If your scope is a specified 200 major journals on the subject, what portions of those journals will be covered? Complete cover-to-cover inclusion in either a bibliographic or full text database is very unusual. A decision must be made and documented as to what type of information in each journal will be included or excluded.

Common criteria for inclusion or exclusion include subject matter, type of information, length, and quality. For example, the producer of a bibliographic database that covers 200 journals may decide to exclude letters to the editor, book reviews, and advertisements in those journals. Many go further and exclude editorials, articles less than a certain length, or articles judged to be of peripheral interest or of poor quality. Newspaper databases often exclude local weather reports, sport scores, recipes, and ship sailings.

Sometimes database producers set different criteria for different publications. For a core of 50 journals, for example, all information except advertisements may be covered, for another group of 150 titles, however, only lengthy articles dealing directly with the subject of the database will be included.

Some database producers choose to state the extent of their coverage positively in terms of what is included in the database rather than what is excluded. A positive statement may be, for example, "This database covers all articles in the specified journals that are over 1,000 words and that discuss some aspect of tropical agriculture." It is probably clearest to state both inclusions and exclusions. An example of a highly selective extent of coverage statement for a local newspaper index is given in Figure 5.2.

Just as with scope decisions, your extent of coverage decisions both deny access to certain items and provide a filter to an overabundance of information. The needs and desires of the users should be uppermost in making such decisions and should be a direct outgrowth from the needs analysis.

FIGURE 5.2   Extent of Coverage for the Hawaii Newspaper Database

Final editions of two Honolulu newspapers, the Star-Bulletin and the Advertiser, are indexed in the Hawaii Newspaper database. Everything in the newspapers is not indexed; an attempt is made to be highly selective and include only those things that have the most long-term interest to the people of Hawaii. Selection of items for inclusion is made at the discretion of the indexers according to the following criteria:

1. Current events, issues and features with information that will have an impact on the future (e.g., planning issues, ordinances, court rulings, legislation, etc.). Articles containing historical information.
2. Individuals: Local interviews or feature articles on well-known personalities or politicians. Include local interviews of mainland celebrities only with substantial information.
3. Business: Articles with biographical information on executive appointments to large local companies. Articles featuring local businesses. Disregard Business Indicator column, Business Digest column, and companies' quarterly earnings.
4. Crime: Articles of front page significance and those articles when victims and accused are named.
5. Trials: For major trials include articles on the trial's opening, final verdict, and major turn of events during trial.
6. Accidents, fires, etc.: Front page articles or unusual articles where victims are named.
7. Sports: Local championship games, major and locally sponsored races and/ or tournaments. Feature articles on local athletes, coaches, or sport figures.
8. Cookery: only local foods or recipes of prominent local persons, families, restaurants, bakeries, etc.
9. Reviews: Include art exhibit reviews, book reviews on Hawaii and Pacific

area subjects, drama reviews of local theater groups, local opera reviews, television or motion pictures, or phono-recordings by local performers or about Hawaii. Entertainment reviews include dance, musical concerts, etc. Disregard reviews of cabaret shows and Honolulu Symphony Orchestra without guest performers.

10. Pacific Area: All articles that pertain to the Pacific area. May be written by local journalists or syndicated wire services.
11. Letters to editor: Controversial topics written by well-known personalities or government officials. Disregard letters written by the general public.
12. Editorials: Memorials of deceased individuals.
13. Religion: Articles featuring local religious persons and/or churches. Church activities or celebrations with historical information.
14. Conferences: Local conferences' keynote speakers. Disregard articles that deal with what went on in the conference unless it is of local significance.
15. Entertainment: Articles that give biographical information on entertainment personalities. Feature articles on plays, musicals, dance groups, musical groups, etc.
16. Obituaries: All Honolulu Advertiser obituaries will be indexed. Star-Bulletin obituaries of prominent people will be indexed only if substantially different.

(Thanks to the Hawaiian-Pacific section of the Hawaii State Library.)

Editions

What editions of a work to include is a primary concern only when a bibliographic or full text database covers newspapers. Many newspapers have morning and evening editions, or early and final editions, or even west coast and east coast editions. For an inhouse database the decision of which edition to use must be made based on the edition most accessible to your users. It is merely a decision that must be made, documented, and consistently applied if possible.

Country of Origin

Few of us realize how many national biases we bring to the provision of access to information. Even commercial database producers often claim "worldwide" coverage while excluding items from entire nations or regions. (See Byrne.)

With an inhouse database, the issue may be easier to resolve since the needs of the users will always be the primary determining factor for all content decisions. In addition to the users' stated desires, the availability of foreign items must be considered as well as the areas of the world that are applicable to the subject matter covered in your database. It is less and less acceptable in today's world to exclude the literature of an entire region through ignorance or mere convenience. Too much valuable information may be lost. Figure 5.3 is an example of the foreign items policy of an inhouse database.

Language

Closely related to country of origin is, of course, the language of the items to be covered in a database. The language of source items may be the primary reason a certain nation's literature is excluded from some databases. Language is addressed as well as country of origin in Figure 5.3.

Once again, this is a practical consideration that must be decided by the database creator and users of the database. You must balance the availability of the foreign language items, the ability of your users to read them, the availability of translations, the costs of acquiring and dealing with foreign language items with the need to provide access to all information on a topic. In the feasibility study you discovered what languages were covered in the collection. Before proceeding with the database, you should reevaluate that coverage and determine if changes should be made. The resulting decisions should be documented as a well thought-out decision.

Full Text

If your collection consists of printed documents, one of the early decisions to be made is whether to include the full texts or just a bibliographic surrogate of these documents in your database. A majority of publicly available textual databases still contain only document surrogates.

Bibliographic databases became the norm for several practical reasons. Computer storage space was too expensive and too limited to accommodate large volumes of text, plus the cost of retrospectively converting full texts was prohibitive. With the decreasing costs and increasing capacity of computer storage, full text databases are becoming increasingly available on commercial search systems. Mead Data Central's LEXIS and NEXIS systems are massive databanks composed of hundreds of full text files. The online vendors BRS and DIALOG, once vendors of bibliographic databases only, now each include many full text databases.

In the microcomputer environment also, full text databases are now a possibility. The database creator must consider several factors

Figure 5.3   Language and Country of Origin Statements from the Tuna Fish Database

---

The Tuna Fish database includes worldwide research items on any species of tuna fish. Items in any language will be considered for inclusion, but English language items typically are indexed more quickly. Items in English or with English language summaries are included immediately; some foreign language items will need to be sent to a translation service before they can be indexed.

A special effort is made to collect and index Asian language items. A cooperative agreement with several universities in Japan insures that the Japanese literature is identified and included.

---

when deciding whether to include the full text of documents or to limit the database to bibliographic information only.

Users' needs. Will users have access to the complete documents in printed form that are retrieved in a bibliographic search? If not, how important is the timeliness of access? Are the printed documents readily available in more than one place?

Primary purpose of the database. Is bibliographic control over the literature of a particular subject or region the primary aim of your database? Is document retrieval and access more important? Do you feel responsible for providing complete texts of documents retrieved or does your responsibility end with letting users know of the existence of material?

Nature of the material. Are the documents written in a precise or specialized language that will make full text searching more successful (e.g., laws or technical materials)? Are facts embedded in documents that can only be retrieved by a full text search? Are pictures, charts, and graphs an important part of the documents, so that printed versions would be needed even if texts were online? Do the texts contain many specialized characters not found on a standard computer keyboard? Are the texts in English?

Permission from publishers. Are the documents copyrighted by someone other than yourself or your organization? If so, can you get the necessary permission from the copyright holders?

Even if the answers to all of the preceding questions indicate that full text is desirable, there are two practical considerations that may preclude its use at the present time.

Conversion. Is the full text now in machine readable form? If so, can it easily be edited to match your software requirements? If not, how will you convert it? (See Chapter 9.) The cost, time, and editing required may be prohibitive for large-scale conversion projects.

Machine storage. To estimate the disk capacity required for a full text database, complete the following calculation: number of documents in collection times average number of words per document times average number of characters per word (including a blank space for every word). This will give you an estimate of the character (byte) requirements just to store the text. Space required by the software for the overhead of inverted indexes will vary from 50 percent to 500 percent.

If a full text database includes 1,000 articles averaging 5,000 words per article and six letters per word, a 30 megabyte (30,000,000 characters) disk drive is needed just to store the text. That requirement will easily be doubled for inverted indexes. On the other hand, a bibliographic database pointing to these same articles could easily fit in one megabyte (plus overhead).

This picture may not be as gloomy as it sounds. Storage capacities of disk drives for microcomputers are increasing at a steady rate, while the costs of these drives continue to come down. More texts are created using computers, and advances in the technology of optical character recognition (OCR) will make widespread conversion of printed texts more possible in the future. If your feasibility study suggests you should consider a full text database, it might be planned for in the near future. In the meantime, bibliographic surrogates can substitute.

Some inhouse databases have started with bibliographic data and added full text at a later date. A litigation support database, for example, includes bibliographic records from 1975–1985. Items from 1986 on are full text. The full text records include all of the information found in the bibliographic style records with the addition of fields for all text paragraphs and references.

Whether your database is bibliographic only, full text only, or a combination, the same decisions regarding value-added fields must be made. For more information on full text databases, see the articles by Tenopir in the Further Readings section of this chapter.

STRUCTURAL DECISIONS

The most important early structural decisions you will make in your database design will be whether or not to standardize input in any way or to add intellectually created value-added fields. Later structural decisions will lay out all of the fields to be included and their order, characteristics, and size. These decisions will be discussed in detail in Chapter 6, but they rely on decisions described here.

A *value-added field* is defined here as any field added to the records in a database for the purpose of improving retrieval or enhancing the record. It is usually done by human intellectual effort, although computers can help in some minor ways, and there are many experimental instances of major computer assistance. So called value-added fields increase the cost of creating a database but improve retrieval. Standardization of input involves human or computer-assisted examination of the contents of specified fields to make sure the values are translated into a correct form or format.

As the creator of a database, even an inhouse database, you must balance the cost at creation and input in terms of time, maintenance, and intellectual effort of personnel with the benefits at output for the users. The decision should be made early in the design process as a direct outgrowth of the feasibility study, as it is almost always more difficult and more expensive to go back and add value-added fields or standardize input after your database has been created.

Standardization

Some commercial database producers fail to standardize any fields at input. Instead of, for instance, always referring to an author by last name, comma, first name, middle initial, period, they input names in a variety of formats with inconsistent punctuation. If you search publicly available databases, you know how frustrating this can be for the user. The lack of simple standardization adversely affects retrieval because almost all information retrieval systems are extremely literal. Most systems cannot tell that Jones, E is really the same person as Jones E. or Jones, Ernest R.

The inhouse database producer must weigh the effort involved to standardize against the benefits for the user. Standardization must be considered early in the design process because it will affect field definition, software evaluation, and the time required to maintain a database. Some areas that are candidates for standardization include dates, citations, names, places, abbreviations, and spelling. (Subject descriptors are discussed later under Indexing.)

Publication dates of items can be input in many different ways. A year can be entered as 1985 or 85 or as part of a more precise date (e.g., 09/17/85 or 85/17/09). Months can be spelled out, abbreviated, or entered as numbers. In most textual databases there will be a variety of types of dates. Books will have only a year, journals may have a month and year or season and year (e.g., Summer 1985), newspapers may have a month, day, and year.

You will find that some software have built-in date features that dictate how dates should be entered or that automatically convert date formats. Before you look at these packages, you should have examined your items to discover the range of date types and to make decisions on how they should best be handled to meet your needs.

If users need to search by year, it is recommended that year be treated as a separate field and be input in the natural way (i.e., 1985). Input of month, day, and year should be standardized also, but usually only if your needs analysis revealed the necessity of searching and retrieving by them. In this instance, converting to numbers may be necessary if range searching is desired (e.g., everything published between January 1985 and September 1985).

Citation information including publisher, volumes, and issues should be standardized if it will be needed for retrieval or for production of formatted reports. In many databases this information is not made searchable or sortable, and standard reports (e.g., bibliographies) are not required. Instead, the citation is provided just for reference, so standardization is not so crucial. Even if this information is only used for reference, however, standardization will affect the length of required fields (volume 1 vs. v1) and ease of readability.

Names of people, whether used as authors, subjects, or directory entries, are candidates for standardization. Users of commercial databases realize how frustrating it can be to try to second guess a database as to whether or not first names are listed as initials or in full and with what punctuation. Something as trivial as a comma placed after an inverted last name will affect retrieval in most of the systems in use today.

Standardization of names can be as simple as having input rules such as last name, comma, space, first name, space, middle initial (if any), period. Library catalogs typically have treated authors' names much more elaborately by creating "authority files," which list the proper form of every name used in the catalog with cross references from alternate forms. Authority files ensure consistency, but are time-consuming to maintain. They are of most use in very large databases, where browsing through an alphabetic list of names is difficult.

Many inhouse database creators choose to follow simple standard rules, rather than create authority files. Software can be selected that will allow alphabetic browsing through the entries in the name field to ensure consistency at input and to aid searching.

Place names can be standardized for ease of retrieval either as a part of a citation (place of publication), as a separate field (geographic location or address in a referral database), or within abstracts or texts. The most common reason to standardize places is if the place is to be a separate searchable field that is particularly important in your database. Since this is the case in a referral or directory database, standardized geographic locations should always be considered for these databases. Standardization in abstracts or texts is rarely done.

The most common standardization for place is to use the two-letter post office code for U.S. states and territories. An authority file for foreign countries will probably be necessary. Standardization of places also includes the decision of level of enrichment. If a document indicates Chicago, will you add IL so searchers can access all information within the state of Illinois? Will you also add United States so searchers can access all information from a country? Are other geographic designations more appropriate (e.g., mid-western U.S.)?

Obviously, these decisions depend on the purpose of your database, how it will be used, and how much other information is available for searching. Some geographic standardization may be considered as subject descriptors (discussed later). Automatic hierarchical term expansion using an online thesaurus as described in Chapter 3 would be a way to automatically include all geographic levels. Any standardization or addition of such information slows down input, but aids retrieval.

Abbreviations and spelling are the other aspects of input standardization that greatly affect retrieval. Different use of acronyms or variations in spelling by authors can make it difficult to locate needed information in a database. Spelling differences are a particular problem in databases that contain information from different countries. For example, information may be carried as the author spells it or changed to American or British spelling. Standardizing at the input stage, however, is a time-consuming process. If an inputter has to double check a list or a dictionary throughout the input stage, the input process is greatly slowed and errors are bound to creep in.

Database producers typically decide to leave spelling as in the original document for fields such as title, abstracts, and full text. The burden of rectifying spelling variations or errors rests with the searcher.

If the database users are unused to the literal nature of database searching and are unlikely to consider spelling variations, a better alternative is to have the software do some of the standardization. For their full text systems (LEXIS and NEXIS) Mead Data Central's software includes "look-up" tables for acronyms, government agencies, plurals and singulars, variations between British and American spelling, and variations between Chinese romanization schemes. Full texts are input as the author wrote them, but during the search process the software automatically checks a user's query to see if an alternate spelling should be searched in the texts. The computer does the checking automatically and transparently for the user. It is rare for microcomputer software to have such a sophisticated feature, but the software evaluator should be aware of the possibility before examining software.

All standardization decisions are essentially ones of quality control that balance the extra time required at input with the time required and success rate at output. The decisions will vary greatly from one inhouse database to the next, depending on human resources available, needs and sophistication of users, and availability of special features in the software you evaluate.

Value-Added Fields

The addition of value-added fields to your database is an even more important decision that must be weighed in much the same way. The most common value-added fields are subject descriptors and abstracts. Others might be codes for indicating such things as Standard Industrial Classification, biological processes, events, and so on. In some sense, any standardization at input (e.g., IL for Illinois) adds intellectual value, but the discussion here is limited to fields added. Part 2 of Appendix A shows how the value-added decisions were made for one inhouse database.

INDEXING

Subject descriptors (also called index terms or subject headings) have typically been added to bibliographic databases to increase the number of search access points. This may be especially important when, for example, the titles of the articles in a reprint collection are relatively short or are not descriptive of content. Subject descriptors may also serve to provide consistent, controlled subject access to supplement free text searching of title words, abstract words, or words in complete texts. This implies the existence of some sort of controlled vocabulary or thesaurus that lists acceptable forms of words or phrases and provides rules for adding terms. Indexers choose terms that describe the subject of a document from this approved list. Cross references from unapproved forms to the correct form are provided.

Indexing requires skills and time that will increase the cost of your database project. The time lag between publication of a document or article and the time the intellectual analysis is complete and it can be input into your database may be unacceptable. As a database designer, you will need to decide whether or not to add a subject descriptor field.

Term Authority Lists

If you decide to add subject descriptors to your database, there are a series of decisions that must be made. The first of these is whether or not to control the terms in some way. The simplest form of indexing is done by merely adding natural language words or phrases as they are used in the texts of the documents. The language of the original authors is preserved, and the objective of adding more retrieval points is met. Because indexers do not consult a list of approved terms, this type of indexing may be done quickly, but term format and use may be inconsistent.

It is often better to keep some control over word forms in subject indexing. Controlled vocabulary indexing means that you use some sort of term authority list and rules for formation of terms. It provides more consistency and therefore improved retrieval, ensuring, for example, that a singular or plural form of a word is always used. Controlled vocabulary indexing requires more work and control at the input stage, but allows less effort at the searching stage. It requires compiling and maintaining some type of word list that indexers follow. Alternatives for controlled vocabulary indexing vary from merely maintaining a list of terms used so indexers can verify word form to creating a highly structured thesaurus.

Maintaining a list of terms used (term authority list) is a simple way to provide indexing consistency, but provides no help in the intellectual process of describing a subject. Indexers select subject terms as they examine documents, but verify the correct forms in the term authority list before assigning the terms. New terms may be manually or automatically entered into the list. You will probably want to add simple cross reference structure to the term authority list, adding SEE or USE references from unused word forms to

FIGURE 5.4   Sample Portion of a Term Authority List

AGING	AIR POLLUTION
AGITATION	AIR SAFETY
AGREEMENTS	AIR TRAFFIC CONTROL
AGRIBUSINESS	AIRCRAFT
AGRICULTURAL	AIRLINES
AGRICULTURAL	AIRPORTS
COMMODITIES	ALCOHOL
AGRICULTURAL	ALCOHOLISM
ECONOMICS	ALGORITHMS
AGRICULTURAL	ALIENATION
PRODUCTION	ALIENS
AGRICULTURE	ALLOCATIONS
AIR	ALLOWANCES
AIR CONDITIONING	ALLOYS
AIR FARES	ALPHABETICAL FILING
AIR FORCE	ALPHANUMERIC FILING
AIR FREIGHT SERVICE	ALUMINUM

correct forms. For an example of a simple term authority list, see Figure 5.4.

Formulating some simple rules will help you to add new terms more consistently. For example, you might decide that plural forms of words will be favored over singular (MICE rather than mouse) and that the gerund form of verbs will be favored (WELDING rather than weld). For geographic names, the standardization rules discussed earlier may be used.

Another decision is to what degree will *precoordinate* terms be used in the vocabulary. Precoordination is the act of putting words together at input to describe subjects. The simplest form of precoordination is to use multiple word terms rather than a series of single words. For example, COMPUTER AIDED DESIGN would be used rather than COMPUTERS and DESIGN. More complex precoordination involves adding subfields to descriptors (GREAT BRITAIN—TRAVEL AND TOURISM). Precoordination retains the intellectual description of a subject, but may add more characters to the descriptor field and can get confusing to users if there are many levels of precoordination. How much precoordination you use in part depends on the software selected. Software suited for textual databases should allow you to retain the precoordination relationships (phrase parsing), but also allow searchers to look for the individual component words within a precoordinated string (word parsing). Searching for individual words

FIGURE 5.5   Sample Portion of a Thesaurus

INFORMATION BROKERS
    SN   Independent information specialists who retrieve, organize and disseminate information for payment.
    BT   Information Services

INFORMATION NEEDS
    RT   Needs Evaluation
           Inquiries
           Search Strategies
    BT   Needs
Information Processing
    USE DATA PROCESSING

INFORMATION SERVICES
    SN   Includes works on creating, collecting, organizing, retrieving, and disseminating of information.
    BT   Services
    NT   Current Awareness Services
           Data Processing
           Information Brokers
           Reference Services

INFORMATION SYSTEMS
    RT   Data Processing
           Online Searching
    NT   Decision Support Systems
           Management Information Systems
           Storage and Retrieval Systems

---

and linking them in the search phase is called *postcoordination*. The best software allows both pre- and postcoordination.

Thesaurus Use

Subject authority lists allow simple vocabulary control in small databases. It is difficult to be consistent when these lists get long, however, because they provide no intellectual help in identifying related, narrower, or broader concepts. You may want to consider using a more sophisticated controlled vocabulary aid such as a thesaurus. Figure 5.5 shows a portion of a typical thesaurus.

The advantages of a thesaurus for controlled vocabulary indexing include:

- controls synonyms by providing cross references from unacceptable terms to acceptable terms
- controls word forms (e.g., singulars and plurals)
- controls homographs (words that are spelled the same, but have different meanings, such as "plant")
- provides a hierarchical structure indicating broader, narrower, and related relationships between terms
- helps an indexer to apply terms consistently
- provides pre-coordinated multi-word terms and rules for further pre-coordination
- explains how terms should be used and resolves ambiguities through scope notes
- provides rules and procedures for assigning terms
- may provide rules for adding new terms to the thesaurus

But there also are disadvantages to using a thesaurus. It may not reflect new terms or recent changes in vocabulary, it may use word forms that seem unnatural to the user, it requires skilled personnel to do the indexing, therefore increasing the cost of database production, and it may slow down the data input procedures as documents are held for indexing.

The process of devising the controlled vocabulary thesaurus from scratch is time-consuming and can be expensive. Inhouse database producers have several options that are simpler than creating a new thesaurus. These options are to adopt a commonly used thesaurus, adapt an existing thesaurus, or adapt a portion of several existing thesauri.

Adopt a thesaurus. Depending on the subject of your database, you can use a thesaurus that has already been created. Your staff or users may already be familiar with a thesaurus used in a publicly available database or indexing publication, making it an easy matter to extend its use to your project. For example, *Medical Subject Headings* (MeSH) might be appropriate for a medical database, the *ERIC Thesaurus* for an education or library database, or *Subject Headings for Engineering* (SHE) for an engineering database.

There are hundreds of thesauri available and on virtually every topic. (See Further Readings for directories that list thesauri available worldwide.) Adopting a good existing list has certain advantages:

- you are spared the cost and effort of creating your own
- users may already be familiar with an existing thesaurus
- your database will be consistent with other retrieval tools

- you may be able to use someone else's indexing for records in your database
- the list has been created by experts in thesaurus construction and/ or the subject matter

But there are disadvantages to this option as well. A thesaurus may not exist for the exact subject of your database; a published thesaurus is already out-of-date in some fields, new terms will not be reflected, some existing terms may sound archaic; the terms may not reflect how your users think or speak; and the level of specificity may be too great or not great enough for your database.

Adapt a Thesaurus. A better plan for an inhouse database may be to find an existing thesaurus that most closely matches your needs and adapt it for your users. Adding or changing terms as needed, providing extra cross references, or choosing only a subset of an existing thesaurus will allow you to utilize the advantages of an existing thesaurus without many of the disadvantages. In many cases the rules for terms in the thesaurus will be adequate. You will be able to follow established rules with clear guidelines when new terms need to be added. The doctors in the case study in Appendix A chose to use MeSH, modified with local terms and preferences.

Adapt Portions of Thesauri. If no one thesaurus sufficiently covers your topic, you may wish to borrow terms from several thesauri. This has the advantage of providing you with authoritative terms in different subjects. It is an especially useful tactic with multidisciplinary topics that are not covered in any one authoritative list. You must, however, reconcile different word form conventions or rules.

Create Your Own. The final and most time-consuming alternative is to create your own thesaurus from scratch. With a custom-built thesaurus you will be better able to match the terms used in your collection and by your users. It is a process that requires a logical mind and some practice to do correctly. There are national and international standards for thesaurus construction (ANSI-American National Standards Institute—Z39.19, 1974 and ISO-International Standards Organization—2788 and 5964). Lancaster and Soergel provide specific instructions on thesaurus construction.

Deciding on Controlled Vocabulary

Your decision on where to turn to for controlled vocabulary terms should be made considering several factors. These factors include:

- what thesauri now exist covering the topic of your database,
- how well constructed these thesauri are (Do they follow the national and international standards?),
- how up-to-date they are,
- what terms your users are accustomed to,
- the uniqueness of your documents, and
- your budget.

Rules

In addition to deciding where index terms come from, you will need to devise some rules for input. A good thesaurus not only provides a term list and cross reference structure, it includes rules for creating new terms and for assigning terms to documents. As a database designer, if you choose to use controlled vocabulary indexing, you will have to decide whether to adopt existing rules or to create new ones. In addition, you will need to make decisions about the number of terms assigned per document, the level of terms assigned, whether index terms will all be input into one field or whether they will be in separate fields by type of subject, who will do the indexing, policies for adding new terms, and policies for precoordination.

Often in a manual system there are stringent rules as to the number of index terms that can be assigned. These rules were usually formulated for very practical reasons—too many index terms resulted in too many catalog cards or too many pages in a printed book. These concerns are not as important in a database (although the more terms used the greater the amount of storage space used). In fact, some publishers of publicly available databases, who also publish printed indexes, include more terms in the online file than in the printed product. Beware of arbitrary limits on the number of terms, but realize that more terms may increase the time involved to index, input, and search.

Related to the number of terms is the level of terms assigned. Standard library cataloging practices dictate that terms are assigned based on the level of specificity of the document being indexed. If an article is a general one on all breeds of cats, for example, the broad term *cats* will be assigned, but not a term for each specific breed. For an article on Siamese Cats, on the other hand, the term *Siamese cats* will be used, but not the broader single term *cats*. In some sense this will depend on the vocabulary you are using. The depth and breadth of vocabularies varies and should match the size, depth, and breadth of your collection. When selecting an existing list of terms, you must take this into consideration.

An inhouse database creator can make his or her own rules. You may wish to follow standard practice, but more often rules should be made based on the identified needs of the users. In some instances both the general and specific terms are useful. A database providing access to a land development firm's tract maps, for example, may need to index on the specific level of each map while also adding the general geographic location. One building in a tract may receive subject headings describing that building as well as subject headings describing the entire tract. Users can thus find all the maps that have anything to do with the tract. Let your users' needs dictate rules for level of indexing.

Index terms may all be placed in a single value-added field labeled *subjects,* or *descriptors,* or the like. Here you will place any added term, whether it is a subject term, a geographic location, a company product, and so on. This is the simplest approach if your users are likely to think of all of these terms as subjects and to search for any category. If, however, some of your users think of these as separate entities and may only search on one type of information, you might want to create several value-added fields. The decision should be made based on how most users are likely to think of subjects and be likely to look for information.

The indexer may have a role in this decision also. If the indexer needs to consult different authority lists or thesauri for different types of information, you might set up separate fields. If the indexer is accustomed to a single field for subjects as is typical in library card catalogs or commercial databases, it may be better to make your inhouse database consistent with these tools.

The capabilities of the indexer should also have a bearing on your decisions regarding adding new terms and pre-coordinating old ones. An inexperienced or clerical indexer may feel uncomfortable adding new terms or following elaborate rules of pre-coordination. Some inhouse database producers allow new terms to be added only if such a term is encountered several times in the literature or if a higher authority (person or printed work) approves. This may help retain the integrity of the vocabulary list, but will not accurately reflect document contents or current terminology. Each situation may differ.

Automatic Help

So far this discussion of controlled vocabulary indexing implies a human indexer assigning terms from a printed list. The terms are attached to a record representing a document and input into the database. The computer assists only with the mechanics of input and at the point of search and retrieval. Automatic indexing has been the focus of many research studies for over 20 years, but is as yet rarely used in practice. (See Borko, Lancaster, and Salton and McGill.)

There are, however, different levels of computer assistance in the indexing process, some of which you may be able to include in an inhouse database. These levels are discussed from the simplest and most widely available in the information retrieval software now on the market to the most complex and least widely available:

1. Online display of terms available for searching is achieved by allowing a portion of the inverted index of the database to be viewed. This allows a human indexer to see if a term has been used previously and to view correct word form. Usually no cross references are present.
2. Online display of a thesaurus shows a separate file that contains a complete thesaurus including cross references and hierarchical structure.
3. Using automatic mapping, if an indexer enters an unaccepted descriptor term for which a cross reference has been provided, the system will automatically substitute the correct term.
4. Automatic controlled vocabulary indexing by word frequency or term weighting, although found in experimental systems, is allowed by few databases.

If any of these levels of computer assistance in indexing are important to you, you will need to include them in your software evaluation process. The more sophisticated features will limit your software options and are at the present time usually available only in the more expensive packages. You might wish to evaluate them as a desirable, but not essential, feature. Availability of these features on specific software packages will be described in more detail in Chapter 7.

Indexing Summary

The inhouse database producer has four basic decisions in regard to controlled vocabulary: whether to offer controlled vocabulary indexing, what thesaurus to use, what policies to develop, and what automatic aids to look for in software.

Controlled vocabulary indexing can make searching easier and more consistent, but it requires added time and therefore costs at input and for maintenance. The producer must therefore balance the benefits to the users with the time involved. Some things a database producer can do to reduce the costs of controlled vocabulary indexing include: choosing a good thesaurus at the beginning of the design process that matches the subject, depth and breadth of your documents, having clear instructions and policies for indexers, and using automatic aids as much as possible within the limits of the software.

ABSTRACTS

After index terms, abstracts are the most common value-added field in bibliographic databases. In a bibliographic database an abstract can serve as a substitute for the document itself, it provides more retrieval points if each word is searchable, and it facilitates judging the relevance of a document to a query. In a full text database it has less value, but may still be useful for purposes of relevance judgment.

An abstract is ideally an accurate and concise summary of a document's contents. An abstract typically has 100 to 300 words, although the database creator has control over the length.

Harold Borko and Charles L. Bernier's *Abstracting Concepts and Methods* is an excellent book that is highly recommended for those who are considering including abstracts in their database. They define abstracts through three characteristics: brevity, accuracy, and clarity. They cite brevity because an abstract eliminates redundant words, chooses important words, and uses standard abbreviations; accuracy because an abstract reflects the original document's content; and clarity because abstracts are written clearly and in a readable style.

The purpose and style of abstracts can vary with the purpose of a database. The four major types are *informative, indicative, critical,* and *special purpose*. Informative abstracts are intended to substitute for the original document and often include a summary of findings and/or parts of tables. Indicative, or descriptive, abstracts tell the reader what she or he will find in the original document. Critical, or review, abstracts provide evaluation of the contents of a document, including the abstractor's opinion on its quality and worth. Special purpose abstracts are geared to a specific group of users and relate information of interest to them. Special purpose abstracts are useful in inhouse databases. For example, the abstracts for a pharmaceutical firm's databases can concentrate on the portion of a document that mentions substances used in the experiments conducted by that firm. Examples of all four types of abstracts are given in Figure 5.6. The special purpose abstract may have been written for a chemical firm.

FIGURE 5.6   Four Types of Abstracts

Tenopir, Carol. *Retrieval Performance in a Full Text Journal Article Database.* Ph.D. dissertation, University of Illinois, 1984.

INFORMATIVE:
The study compared results from searching the full text of journal articles in the Harvard Business Review Online database on the BRS system with the results from searching on the titles and the value-added fields of abstract and controlled vocabulary. There was a significant difference at the .05 level between the full text and other methods for total documents retrieved, recall ratio, and overlap/ uniqueness of specific documents retrieved. Word occurrence patterns were shown to be meaningful in full texts. If a search word occurs 1-5 times in a text there was a mean 12.6% precision ratio; 6-10 times a 29.2%; 11-15 times a 55%; 16-20 times a 66.7%; and 21-25 a 72.7% precision ratio. If search words occurred in four or more text paragraphs the documents were 58% relevant on the average, compared to 11.5% for one paragraph.

INDICATIVE:
The study compared results from searching the full text of journal articles in the Harvard Business Review Online database on the BRS system with the results from searching on the titles and the value-added fields of abstract and controlled vocabulary. There was a significant difference between the full text and other methods for total documents retrieved, recall ratio, and overlap/uniqueness of specific documents retrieved. Other measures tested included precision ratio and the number of times that words occurred in texts and in text paragraphs. Implications for searchers and database producers are given.

CRITICAL:
The study compared results from searching the full text of journal articles in the Harvard Business Review Online database on the BRS system with the results from searching on the titles and the value-added fields of abstract and controlled vocabulary. Full text searches were limited to word occurrence within the same grammatical paragraph. Results should be interpreted cautiously because only one database on one search system was examined. The language used in Harvard Business Review articles and their controlled vocabulary may not allow generalizations to other subjects or journals. The work was continued by Jung Soon Ro at Indiana University.

SPECIAL PURPOSE:
The study compared results from searching the full text of journal articles in the Harvard Business Review Online database on the BRS system with the results from searching on the titles and the value-added fields of abstract and controlled vocabulary. It includes a section that describes full text databases currently online including the American Chemical Society (ACS) files. Studies of users of ACS files are described, notably results that show chemists use full text to find facts that may be too small a part of the total text to be reflected in index terms, and that once an article is located online users prefer to go to the printed copy of the journal.

If you decided that abstracts will be useful in your database, you next must decide how they will be created. Abstracts can be written by the authors of the original documents, by subject experts, or by professional abstractors. For an inhouse database abstracts can be created by the database staff or taken from a published source depending on the type of abstract desired, the staff available, and the availability of a published abstract. Some journals include an abstract for every article. Abstracts on commercial databases can be downloaded to your computer within the constraints of copyright law. (See Chapter 9 for a further discussion of downloading records.)

As with indexing there have been many experiments with computer based abstracting or extraction. In reality, most abstracts are still written by humans. Many studies show that the first and last sentences in a paragraph are most indicative of content, but experiments have used a variety of methods for automatic selection of important sentences or fragments.

Computerized abstracting is not sufficiently precise and is too complex to be useful for most inhouse databases. The text must be completely in machine readable form, a significance criteria must be developed, the text must then be computer analyzed, and, finally, extracted sentences must be formatted and verified. Advances in computer technology and the possibility of full text databases have made this process of computer extracting less important and, perhaps, obsolete.

There are several alternatives to abstracts that still provide many of the advantages. An *annotation* may be added to a title or to a bibliographic citation as a way of enriching an uninformative title or briefly explaining content; a portion of a document may be *extracted* word-for-word and reproduced in a record; or a *summary* or restatement at the end of a text may be reproduced in a summary field.

OTHER VALUE-ADDED FIELDS

Other information may be added to the records in your database to assist retrieval. The need for this information may have been identified in the needs analysis. Frequently numeric classification schemes are used to summarize subject content while maintaining subject relationships; a purely alphabetical subject system often cannot accomplish this.

There are many different types of numeric classification schemes used for different purposes. If your database contains directory information of local companies, for example, the *Standard Industrial Classification* code number may be helpful. The SIC categorizes types of businesses and will allow users to find all businesses of a certain type. BIOSIS uses classification codes and biosystematic codes that may be useful for an inhouse biological database. These codes place biological entities within their genus and species. The National Library of Medicine's classification numbers retain the hierarchical relationship between subjects. The class number for cornea, for example, clearly places it with other parts of the eye.

FURTHER READINGS

Borko, Harold and Bernier, Charles L. *Abstracting Concepts and Methods*. New York: Academic Press, 1975.

Borko, Harold and Bernier, Charles L. *Indexing Concepts and Methods*. New York: Academic Press, 1978.

Byrne, Alex. "How to Lose a Nation's Literature: Database Coverage of Australian Research." *Database* 6 (August 1983): 10–17. Reply by: Brown, Curtis L. "How NOT to Lose a Nation's Literature." *Database* 6 (December 1983): 11–13.

Davis, Charles H. and Rush, James E. *Guide to Information Science*. Westport, Conn.: Greenwood Press, 1979.

Dolan, Donna R. "Offlines: Designing Databases." *Database* 9 (February 1986): 77–82.

Lancaster, F.W. *Vocabulary Control for Information Retrieval*. 2nd ed. Arlington, Va.: Information Resources Press, 1986.

Milstead, Jessica L. *Subject Access Systems: Alternatives in Design*. New York: Academic Press, 1984.

Rowley, Jennifer E. *Abstracting and Indexing*. Hamden, Conn.: Shoe String Press, 1982.

Salton, Gerard and McGill, Michael. *Introduction to Modern Information Retrieval*. New York: McGraw-Hill Book Company, 1983.

Soergel, Dagobert. *Indexing Languages and Thesauri: Construction and Maintenance*. New York: Wiley, 1974.

Soergel, Dagobert. *Organizing Information: Principles of Data Base and Retrieval Systems*. New York: Academic Press, 1985.

Svenonius, Elaine. "Unanswered Questions in the Design of Controlled Vocabularies." *Journal of the American Society for Information Science* 37 (September 1986): 331–340.

Tenopir, Carol. "Full Text Database Retrieval Performance. " *Online Review* 9 (April 1985): 149–164.

Tenopir, Carol. "Full-Text Databases." *Annual Review of Information Science and Technology* 19 (1984): 215–246.

Tenopir, Carol. "Searching Harvard Business Review Online . . . Lessons in Searching a Full Text Database." *Online* 9 (March 1985): 71–78.

Townley, Helen M. and Gee, Ralph D. *Thesaurus-Making: Grow Your Own Word-Stock*. London: Andre Deutsch Ltd., 1980.

Directories of Thesauri

International Classification and Indexing Bibliography: Classification Systems and Thesauri, 1950–1982. Indeks Verlag, 1982.

Thesaurus Guide: Analytical Directory of Selected Vocabularies for Information Retrieval. Amsterdam, North-Holland, 1985.

6
Record Definition and Field Specifications

Once you have completed your feasibility study and formulated your initial editorial decisions, you will be ready to make the structural decisions that will allow your project to crystallize into a structured database. These structural decisions cover: record definition, field definition, and field specifications.

As discussed in Chapter 1 and illustrated in Figures 1.1–1.3, most textual databases divide the contents of the database into units called records. The structure and uniformity of the records will vary with the application. Records are usually further broken down into a collection of fields. There is typically a high degree of regularity of fields within records in the same database. Fields may be further subdivided into subfields.

Each field in a record will contain information that differs from other fields in some way, and in many cases will call for different treatment by the database software. This chapter discusses the process of identifying records and fields and defining their structure, their content types, and how they will be treated by the software.

RECORD DEFINITION

Most of the software discussed in *Managing Your Information* requires the content of the database to be structured into records. How you define a record in your database will depend on the nature of the information and your application. In some cases the definition of the records will be fairly straightforward and obvious, in other cases this breakdown will seem somewhat arbitrary and perhaps forced. For example, in a database containing bibliographic citations, it is not difficult to see each record defined as the information describing a particular book, article, or report. If a reprint collection, for example, contains 5,000 reprints, the database will have a corresponding 5,000 records. Each record will be further subdivided into fields, each of which describes a particular piece of information about an individual article. Typical fields include such things as author, title, source, and date. The case study example in Appendix A shows the field structure of a typical journal article in a bibliographic database.

The record structure of a full text database may not be as obvious. If your database contains the texts of articles from several journals, will each article, each issue, or each journal be a record? If your database is the text of a single book or manual, the text might not provide the same kind of repeating units that naturally can be divided into records. In the latter example, you might define records as chapters, or sections, or paragraphs; further subdivision into fields may not make sense here.

Not all records in every database will be the same. For example, one bibliographic database may include records corresponding to individual journal articles, others might represent an entire book or conference proceeding, still others may describe book chapters. The fields in each of these record types may vary.

A few software packages for textual databases allow different records to be accommodated by having the designer set up a variety of record types, each with a different record structure. The fields in each of these record structures would vary, but the appropriate structure would be selected when inputting data.

More common is the necessity of making a single master record structure that includes all possible fields that would be used by any record type. In this scenario, the inputter must be responsible for selecting and inputting information only in those fields that apply to a particular record type. For example, a bibliographic database might consist of records for books, journal articles, and technical reports. Each type will have some fields that are common to all (e.g., author) and some fields that are unique to the type (e.g., journal title or contract number). By defining a record with fields for all three document types, but entering only those appropriate to each individual item, all these varying record types can be accommodated.

ORGANIZING IN FIELDS AND RECORDS

Some software limits the length of a single record. Even if there are no limits, in most applications the user will want to retrieve a manageable size unit of information. Defining records in a logical way will make the system easier to use and will allow more search features. Record and field definition is ultimately the database designer's choice, as long as it does not exceed software limitations, can be perceived as logical by the users, and is consistently applied.

The idea of organizing information into records and fields is based on the same kind of thinking that caused the development of the printed form. This structure facilitates use of the information and assures uniformity of treatment and the application of standard procedures. For the searcher, the structure allows a greater degree of specificity by limiting the search to specified fields; for the system, the division of the database into records and fields facilitates the generation of indexes and processing of certain portions in specific ways; for the database builder, the structure allows for more convenient inputting and editing. A structured database allows more control of output because portions of a record can be displayed as needed and fields can be arranged as specified. Access can be controlled to a greater degree in the structured database because some software will allow password protection at the field level.

FIELD DEFINITION

After you have determined what will constitute a record in your database, you can begin to define the individual fields within each record. A good place to start is with the "access points needed" section of your feasibility study. In that section you have already determined what parts of the documents are most important for searching; these can now be thought of as fields. If, for example, your users need access by authors, publication year, and subjects, you know you must have an author, date, and subject field. To these fields you may now add any other fields that are necessary to identify an item. In the reprint example, title, citation, and location code may be added. Other value-added fields such as an abstract or a note field may be needed.

Each record should have a unique identifying number for control purposes. Some software will assign this number, some will not. A field for accession number or unique call number should therefore be planned.

Once all of the fields in a database have been determined, you should break them down into the smallest component parts that are needed for searching. Some software will allow you to treat these as subfields, but some will require that you create separate fields for each subunit. Date, for example, may need to be broken down into month and year, if year is to be searched alone. Citation may be subdivided into journal name, volume numbers, and page numbers.

Next, the fields should be arranged in an order that is logical for input. Typically, the unique identifying number comes first, followed by either title or author, all of the citation information, abstract, and subject headings. With some software this input order will be identical to what the searcher sees at output. Other software packages allow the database designer or searcher to customize the output order.

The order of the fields may be dictated by the nature of the information, but in many cases there are options, more than one of which might be reasonable. The sequence should be logical, useful, and convenient for the user. If the sequence that is best for the data entry personnel is not the same as that needed by the database user, then it should be possible to rearrange the data at some point—either at entry or output so that both needs can be met.

FIELD SPECIFICATION

After the fields have been determined, their characteristics must be specified. This process of field specification is the next step in the record structure definition process.

Most database software allows the database designer some flexibility in terms of how each field will be organized and processed by the software. The designer thus needs to make decisions about each field that will ultimately affect the input process, the search power, and the output capabilities of the database. These decisions are discussed below. An illustration for one application appears in Appendix A.

Information for Each Field

The kind of information to be stored in each field, the uses of the information, and the retrieval requirements of the users will dictate certain characteristics that should be specified for each field.

The standard field types are textual (alphanumeric) or numeric. One of the unique characteristics of the databases we are discussing is that most fields will be textual. Author, title, abstract, subjects, and journal name, are all clearly textual. Even fields that contain some numbers, such as volume, issues, and pages, will probably be treated as text, since they require no numeric calculations.

Numeric fields are those that require calculations of some sort. Some fields will be derived from calculations involving other fields. Both of these instances require that the software supports standard mathematical computational abilities.

Other packages allow further subdivision by type of numeric fields into date, currency, and data types. In some cases a date field may be represented either as an alphanumeric value (January 7, 1985) or as a numeric value (19850107 or 850107). The numeric representation offers the advantage of allowing retrieval based on comparison with specified data (e.g., all records with dates after 850101) or sorting in chronological order. The alphanumeric form is more easily understood by the user. Some systems offer both advantages by automatically converting from one form to the other. Currency type fields automatically allow two places after the decimal point, calculate without roundoff errors, and supply the dollar sign (or pound sign) at output. Data type numeric fields may differentiate between integers and real numbers.

Repeating Elements in Fields

Textual databases frequently have fields that may contain repeating elements. Each of the elements is different, but each must be treated equally. One bibliographic record, for example, may include several authors, while the next may have no author. The field for subject descriptors will almost certainly need to accept more than one value, although indexing policy may limit the maximum number.

Many software packages that have been designed for other types of databases cannot deal with multiple values in a field. Typical business applications have only one value per field, unlike textual practice. This specification will serve to eliminate many software packages in the evaluation process.

Values Required for the Field

A document accession number, for example, may be required for each record, whereas an author field may not be needed for all documents. Some software may be able to validate that a value is in each required field. If values will not always be present in some fields, you will probably want to select software that will not reserve space for unused fields and that will not display unused field tags.

Validation of Fields

Some software can use information about each field to provide automatic validation at input. Features that are typically validated include such things as numeric values only in a field or values within a certain range, no dates with more than 31 days in a month, alphabetic characters only, and/or value required. In addition to such simple automatic validation, some fields will need to be controlled with an authority file or thesaurus. The authority file or thesaurus must be checked to provide acceptable terms or term formats. Only a few microcomputer-based software packages are able to do this automatically by using an authority file in machine-readable form. More frequently, the look-up must be done by the person doing the indexing or input.

Security Control at the Field Level

Another level of control is that of security control. Are some fields not to be seen by certain classes of users? Do you want to allow display but not editing capabilities for certain fields for some users? Some kind of user category codes or password control will be needed in the software to handle these kinds of situations. Many of the information retrieval software packages written for single user microcomputers do not provide this kind of security. Most of the packages written for larger, multiuser systems do provide some degree of security at the field level.

Creating Searchable Fields

The fields designated as access points in your feasibility study will obviously need to be searchable. Other fields are useful as searchable fields, however, such as words from titles, words in abstracts, and so on. The database designer needs to decide which fields should be searchable so the software can create the inverted indexes that will make them searchable.

When you decide that a field is to be searchable, you must then decide how it is to be searchable. Should it be word parsed, so every individual word is searchable, but no pre-coordination is maintained? Title and abstract fields are typically word parsed. Should it instead be phrase parsed, so each entire field value is treated as a whole in the inverted index? The author field is frequently phrase parsed to retain the first name, last name relationship. The most powerful option is to designate a combination of word and phrase parsing, so any pre-coordination is maintained but individual words can be searched as well.

Decisions about how the field will be indexed should be based on the retrieval requirements of the users and the search capabilities of the software. You must remember that in most inverted index systems the overhead for indexing may be considerably more than the storage required for the main file. Indexing decisions will have a major impact on this overhead. You will need to balance storage costs and availability with retrieval capability. For example, titles can be indexed by key word and as full titles. A known title could be retrieved by either approach, possibly with some false drops with the key word approach. The cost of eliminating a few false drops for known title searching must be balanced against the cost of generating and storing the full title index. Combination parsing uses the most computer storage space.

Phrase parsing is the most conservative of storage space and is frequently used for the author field. Normally when searching for an author, the user will know the last name and probably the first name or initial. Authors may be conveniently searched with last name and possibly first name truncated (or last name and full first name). This kind of searching is accommodated by phrase parsing of the author field, entering authors into the index as complete names (last, first, middle or with initials). It is unlikely that anyone will want to search on a first name or initial alone.

Fields Used for Sorting Output

The values going into a field that will be used for sorting need to be entered in such a way that a meaningful sort will be produced (e.g., putting an author's last name first). The capabilities of database software packages vary considerably in their ability to produce sorted output. Some offer several options for sorting, such as word by word or letter by letter, leading articles significant or not, numeric values sorted as numbers or as ASCII characters, and so on. They may offer secondary and tertiary sorting if values in the primary sort key are the same. With some packages you may have to buy or write a separate report generator for sorting and formatting of output.

Maximum Lengths of Each Field

In your feasibility study you probably examined characteristics of component parts of your records. One important characteristic is the number of characters needed to describe each component. Lengths of titles, for example, will vary from document to document. The maximum length needed to accommodate title values should be estimated from a random sample of documents. You do not want to average the title lengths of your sample at this point; instead you want to estimate the number of characters that are needed in order to accommodate a vast majority of titles (e.g., 99 percent). The trick is to estimate sufficient room without fixing the figure so high that it is wasteful or unrealistic. Because values may vary a great deal, it may be practically impossible to accommodate 100 percent of the values. For other fields, such as date, it may be easy to estimate maximum lengths.

Estimating maximum lengths will help you to set computer storage requirements and give you a worst case scenario of how much storage space is needed. You will also want to record whether each field is always the same length (fixed length) or varies in size from record to record (variable length). If the fields are variable length, you should note the range of lengths (estimated by examining a random sample of the documents in the collection). Textual databases typically have very few fixed length fields (perhaps accession number and publication year only). If you have many variable length fields with wide ranges in length among documents, you will probably want to select software that does not use fixed length fields. In such variable length software, the average length of a field is a meaningful number for estimating storage requirements.

When you add the estimated maximum field lengths together, you have a base figure for computer storage space required for the linear file portion of your database. To this number will have to be added the *overhead* required by each software package to build inverted indexes or other supporting files. The overhead figure varies from under 50 percent of the base figure to over 500 percent depending on the software package selected; how many fields you have machine indexed; how many values are in each of these fields; and whether each field is word, phrase, or combination parsed.

DOCUMENTING THE DESIGN

During the design process you should keep a record of your decisions and the reasons for them. The process will be based on your earlier feasibility study, which, together with a well organized record of the design process, will contribute to your final system documentation effort. A more immediate use for your design documentation is for the software evaluation and selection process. (While you should go through the record design process before choosing software, you should recognize that some design compromises may be necessary after you have made your software selection.) This step may need to be repeated several times before you decide on a final design.

Field Specification Table

A table covering each field and describing each of the following features is a useful means of summarizing your tentative record design:

Field Tag	Searchable? Word or Phrase?
Field Name	Sortable
Type	Maximum Length
Elements Repeat?	Fixed or Variable
Value Required	Range
Controlled? How?	Average Length

Appendix A shows this table filled in for one application. The tabular information should be supplemented with a more complete narrative description.

Narrative Description

The narrative includes a short description of the *content* of each field. This description may incorporate some policies also, such as stating, "the author field contains the names of all authors of a document," or "the author field contains the names of the first three authors of each document. If there are more than three authors, the first is listed followed by et al."

The *format* of each field describes input rules in more detail or refers to an external authority list. For the author field, the format column might include the rules that authors are recorded as listed on each document with last name, first name, and middle initial. For controlled fields, a reference to the particular authority list or thesaurus should be given. The list might be attached if practical. Examples of how each field will look when the input rules are followed should be supplied.

Data Dictionary

The field specification table and narrative description together form what is known as a *data dictionary*. The data dictionary is created for both computer software and human consumption. The computer-readable data dictionary allows the software to adapt to the record structure, determine the characteristics of each field, and validate input. Software varies as to how much of the information can be handled automatically. Many software packages automate the input of the data dictionary. Field names and characteristics are entered in response to prompts or filling in the blanks on the screen. The information can be printed and used as a part of a human-readable data dictionary.

Even if it is not used by the software, the data dictionary is a valuable aid for the designer and maintainers of the database. It eventually becomes part of the system documentation and procedure manual. Before that, it helps the designer to evaluate and choose appropriate software. Appendix A includes the preliminary data dictionary for the case study.

MULTIPLE FILES

Some applications will require more than one file. This may be desirable if your record types vary considerably so that creating one master record structure becomes too unwieldly. If your users tend to think of different types of information separately (e.g., they search for journal articles, books, or audiovisual materials separately or at different times), you may want to create several different files. You might have an article file, a book file, an audiovisual file, each of which would be designed with a different record structure. Links between these individual files will probably never be necessary.

Other applications require several files, each of which must be linked to the others. This is true in a library environment where you may maintain one file that describes books and another that describes your users. A transaction file would show what books are checked out by what user. This type of need cannot be accommodated merely by creating separate record structures. You will need the file-linking capabilities provided by database management system software or special library applications packages.

FURTHER READINGS

Bates, Ruthann et al. "Innovative Approaches to Database Production: A Case Study on Health Information." In *Proceedings of the Online '83 Meeting,* 1–8. Weston, Conn.: Online Inc., 1983.

Eddison, Betty. "Database Design: Building Strategies for Your Database." *Database* 8 (December 1985): 76–78.

Hlava, Marjorie. *Private File Creation, Database Construction.* New York: Special Libraries Association, 1984.

Norris, Carole L. "Guidelines for Developing an Online In-House Database Through a Commercial Vendor." In *Proceedings of the National Online Meeting,* 435–444. Medford, N.J.: Learned Information, 1982.

Palmer, Roger C. *Online Reference and Information Retrieval.* 2nd ed. Littleton, Colo.: Libraries Unlimited, 1987.

7
Software Options

The success of your inhouse database will ultimately depend on the software selected. Several options in obtaining software for an inhouse database system are purchase ready-to-use applications software (or a turnkey hardware and software system), use generic database management or file management software, or develop custom software using a suitable programming language. For most situations these options would be ranked in the order listed above.

In order to discuss alternatives for software, it is useful to categorize the various packages so that some generalizations can be made before looking at specific packages. We group the software into two main categories: general purpose software, which includes text retrieval software, file managers, and database management systems; and special purpose software, which includes information storage and retrieval software, library automation software, and bibliography generation software. We recognize that there will not be universal agreement as to which category a particular package should be assigned, and the distinctions are not always clear cut between categories. Names and producer addresses for many software packages suitable for textual databases are given in Appendix B.

GENERAL PURPOSE SOFTWARE

Most of the software in this category can be purchased from local computer stores, mail order software distributors, and similar sources. As compared to special purpose software, prices tend to be lower and there is a better chance of finding discounted prices. Support from the producer may not be as strong as for special purpose software, but there is a better chance of finding local or national user groups or informal support groups since these packages, at least the more popular ones, are widely used in a variety of contexts. In this category we include text retrieval software, file management software, and database management systems.

Text Retrieval Software

All of the retrieval packages discussed in this chapter store and retrieve textual data. The software discussed in this section differs from the other categories in that the data is unstructured text rather than organized into fields. If there is structure in the data, it is usually incidental to the functioning of the software. For example, a common application of text retrieval software is for control of word processing files. Some of the files may be letters that will be made up of an address, salutation, body, closing, and name of sender; other files might be minutes of meetings, internal memos, and other documents. Each is treated as a text document and searched based on word occurrence. Some precision is lost due to the lack of structure, but flexibility is added. Being able to handle a variety of document types and the fact that no additional intellectual efforts are made in indexing, abstracting, or reentering the data makes this an appealing approach in some situations.

Text retrieval packages generally offer powerful search capabilities, including Boolean logic, truncation, and word proximity searching. Three examples of this category are ZyINDEX, TEXTBANK, and SearchExpress.

ZyINDEX. ZyINDEX deals with collections of files. Each file might be compared to a record in a regular database or file management system in that it is the basic unit that is retrieved, displayed and processed. Files must be text files, either ASCII or any of several popular word processors' non-ASCII formats.

Files to be included in ZyINDEX must be machine indexed. A user specified or system provided stop word file is used to eliminate noninformative words from the inverted index. Once indexed, files can be searched with Boolean operators, parenthetical grouping of terms, word proximity, truncation, and an internal wild card character. ZyINDEX will display the complete text of the retrieved files and highlights each occurrence of the search terms. The first sixteen lines of the selected text is initially displayed, then the text can be browsed by means of function keys. Portions of the text may be marked and saved in a separate file. Retrieved files or portions of files can be printed.

ZyINDEX comes in four versions: Personal, Standard, Professional, and Plus. The Personal version can handle up to 350 files. The

Standard version can handle up to 500 files and 125,000 unique words in each index; the Professional version supports up to 5,000 files and 125,000 words in the index; and the Plus version supports up to 15,000 files and 500,000 unique words in the index files.

TEXTBANK. TEXTBANK uses a zone concept for data organization and searching. This allows the user to define logical portions of a document (tables, lines, sentences, paragraphs, sections, chapters, and so on) as the focus of the search. Searches may be expanded or limited by "zooming" to larger or smaller zones. TEXTBANK works with any type of information stored in ASCII text files.

Searching features include Boolean operators (OR, AND, NOT, and XOR [exclusive or]); macro term definition (water equals river, or stream, or lake, or canal, or water), which allows the searcher to search for the expanded concept by use of a single term; zone proximity and word proximity searching; and range searching.

Information is displayed on a zone basis so you can view more or less of the document as desired. Scrolling capabilities allow browsing. Results can be sorted, printed, filed, deleted, and undeleted. Some effort is required in defining zones for the particular data in the database. There must be some character or sequence of characters (including control characters) that signals the start of each type of zone.

TEXTBANK occupies less disk space than traditional inverted file systems. Overhead is adjustable (from 50 percent to 150 percent) if disk space is limited.

SearchExpress. SearchExpress is a text retrieval package with several unusual features. In addition to searching with Boolean operators, proximity searching, range searching, comparison searching, and set building, SearchExpress offers some special search features. It supports word searching with user-assigned weights used to rank output, searching for similar documents (presented in order of degree of similarity), and searching for associated or linked documents by user-created links.

SearchExpress works with ASCII text files. As documents are added to the system they are indexed. Overhead for the full version is 50–100 percent. An abbreviated version of SearchExpress offers lower overhead (30–50 percent), but with fewer search options. When indexing and searching SearchExpress automatically strips suffixes from words (e.g., run, runs, runner, and running are equivalent). Indexing can be turned off and on in the text to save overhead by embedding commands in the text.

SearchExpress can handle databases of up to four billion bytes, with up to one million documents per database. Versions to use with CD ROM or Write-once (WORM) optical disks are available.

File Managers

File managers support only a single file. Most of them are relatively simple to use, due in large part to their limited capabilities. They vary considerably in their capabilities and in their cost. Generally, they offer less powerful retrieval capabilities and fewer features when compared to either the generic DBMS or the information storage and retrieval systems discussed later in this chapter. They are marketed for the general user with fairly simple requirements and, for some textual database applications, they can be a good choice. As a group they cost less than the other types of software we have discussed.

Examples of packages in this category that have been used for textual databases include Q & A, DayFlo TRACKER, PFS Professional File, Notebook II, Nutshell, and askSam. Contact addresses for all of these packages are given in Appendix B. Sources for reviews are given in Appendix D. Some of these file managers are discussed briefly below.

Q & A. Q & A integrates word processing with file management. It is notable for its Intelligent Assistant, an artificial intelligence based user interface. The Intelligent Assistant allows the database designer to specify synonyms for the file, for the records, for the fields in each record, and for data elements. This permits users to employ a variety of terms in a query, giving them the power of natural language interaction.

Q & A supports field lengths of up to 1,679 characters and record lengths of up to 16,780 characters with up to 2,400 fields per record, and up to 16 million records per file. Calculated fields are supported and limited programming capabilities are provided in connection with computed or derived field values.

PFS Professional File. PFS Professional File supports fields of up to 1,919 characters, up to 3,200 fields per record, up to 61,000 characters per record, and up to 29,500 records per file. Only the first field is indexed, others are searched sequentially. Calculated fields are supported.

PFS Professional File combines the earlier PFS:File and PFS:Report. It is easy to use and will allow even an inexperienced database designer to design and create a simple database in a few hours. PFS

First Choice is a newer, even simpler version of the integrated package.

DayFlo TRACKER. DayFlo TRACKER is a file manager capable of storing and retrieving a mix of structured and unstructured text. Records with various structures (memos, bibliographic citations, and so on) are all stored in the same file. Variable length fields may be as large as 32,000 characters. Larger blocks of text are divided into multiple records so text of unlimited size can be handled. Up to 101 indexed field values are allowed per record. Multiple values in a field are allowed.

The package includes a basic word processor and a report generator capable of producing textual, columnar, or mixed reports. Retrieval capabilities include truncation and wild card characters, comparison operators, within a range, outside a range, containing or excluding specified values, and with specified fields present or absent.

A convenient command menu on the bottom of the screen together with online help makes this an easy package to learn and use.

Notebook II. Notebook II is menu driven and includes context sensitive help screens. It handles variable length fields and records between 20,000 and 50,000 characters (depending on memory size). Records may be defined with as many as 50 fields.

Data entry is via a screen-oriented editor or by importing files in ASCII or Basic format (Microsoft BASIC, dBASE II system data files, or WordStar mailmerge). A companion program, called Convert, supports the importing of records downloaded from BRS, Dialog, Knowledge Index, or Medline.

Searching features include a find command, which searches for single terms and then displays records in turn that contain the term in a specified field or, optionally, anywhere in the record. The select command supports searching for records that contain, exclude, begin with, do not begin with, or are less than, less than or equal, greater than, or greater than or equal to a term. AND and OR combinations are supported. With set building this allows complex queries to be formulated. A companion program, called Bibliography, produces formatted bibliographies using records in the file and citations in a manuscript.

askSam. askSam is a free format text-oriented file manager with many features. It can deal with collections of unstructured text, or structure may be imposed with fields. askSam recognizes numbers, dates, and telephone numbers and can operate on these to do arithmetic, calendar functions, and automatic phone dialing. Fields may repeat and be in any order, varying from record to record. Records are limited to 20 lines, but longer logical records are easily accommodated as documents (series of linked records). Documents can be any size.

Records may be entered via full screen editor or imported from ASCII files. Templates may be created for each file to define fields, but additional fields may be added as needed.

Search capabilities of askSam include Boolean logic (no parenthetical grouping), comparison, left and right truncation, proximity searching (within a specified number of words, lines, or sentences), and calendar queries.

A hypertext facility supports movement between files, user defined menus, and record linking via words in common. Selected fields may optionally be indexed to speed retrieval in large files.

A programming capability is included, which allows queries and commands to be saved and executed later. A flexible report generator is included, which allows textual or columnar reports.

askSam is powerful, and the user will need to spend some time with it to learn all of its capabilities. It is, however, easy to learn and the basic functions are easy to use. askSam is primarily command driven, so the user manual and the extensive help files are necessary.

Generic Database Management Systems

Database management systems have evolved since the mid 1960s and have been developed primarily in the business environment for business applications. The majority of the DBMS packages on the market suffer from some serious limitations when used for the kind of databases we are considering in this book.

A common limitation is that of being able to deal only with fixed length fields and often with a relatively short upper limit to field lengths. The fixed length field requirement means that each record in the database must be able to accommodate the longest value in the database even though most may be considerably shorter. This will result in wasted storage space and/or truncated field values.

Another common limitation is the inability to accommodate multiple values in fields. For example, in a book record the author field may have anywhere from zero to four or more author names. With a typical DBMS one would be forced to set up a record structure with a set number of authors (e.g., author1, author2, and so on). Books with fewer authors would waste the storage space set aside for the maximum, and books with more than the maximum authors allowed would require some compromise. The problem of multiple field values creates problems for retrieval also in many DBMS in that all values cannot be searched as one field.

The DBMS approach offers several advantages over the file manager approach for certain kinds of applications.

- Multiple files. Data may be kept in several files and these files used simultaneously.
- Data manipulation. Not only can a user search and retrieve from multiple files, he can produce reports that require computation or processing of values in these files.
- Reduced redundancy. A database management system may store data for more than one application, each application seeing only what is needed for that application. Some applications may share certain data.
- Security. Many database management systems offer password protection at several levels.
- Flexibility. Most allow ad hoc queries that may not have been anticipated when the system was set up. Relatively powerful query languages and report generators are common.

Many DBMS offer a built-in programming language that allows more flexibility. The system can be modified to closely match the requirements of a given application. By use of the programming capability, it may be possible to get around some of the limitations of DBMS such as fixed length fields and single values per field. This will require time and expertise in programming.

Examples of generic DBMS packages that might be used for textual databases include dBASE III Plus, R:BASE System V, Paradox, Sequitur, and Revelation.

Fixed Length DBMS. Paradox, dBASE III Plus, and R:BASE System V are similar in their basic capabilities and limitations. Each offers a menu driven user interface, which allows novice users to accomplish useful things with little training. For the experienced user each offers a high level programming language integrated with all of the file handling and query capabilities of the systems.

The dBASE series (II, III, and III Plus) have enjoyed a considerable following in the library community, and there are published programs to perform several library/bibliographic functions in dBASE. Beiser (1987) provides a good introduction to programming in dBASE III Plus for library applications.

Paradox and R:BASE are easier for the novice user. Paradox is based on artificial intelligence technology, and R:BASE works with an optional natural language interface called Clout.

Paradox, dBase, and R:BASE are relational database systems supporting the linking of multiple files. Fields are fixed in length with a maximum of 1,530 characters per field in R:BASE, 255 characters in Paradox, and 254 characters in dBASE III+. R:BASE and dBASE support variable length memo fields of up to 4,096 characters (searchable) in R:BASE System V and 5,000 characters in dBASE III Plus.

Variable Length DBMS. Sequitur integrates word processing with DBMS. It supports variable length fields, with 750 files permitted per database, no limit on records per file, 1,024 fields per record, and no limit to size of a field. The interface is not particularly easy to master, and it has been reported to be slow in performance. The main advantage of Sequitur is its low price of $79.00.

Revelation is a DBMS package that is in a class by itself with regard to its capabilities for textual applications. This system brings the powerful features of the Pick operating system to MS DOS microcomputer systems and adds features that make it more user/programmer-friendly. Notable in Revelation is its ability to deal with variable length fields and records, the number of fields per record supported (65,000), and the upper limit on record size (65,000 characters), file size (no limit), and number of simultaneous files supported (6,000). Revelation offers powerful retrieval capabilities and includes a powerful programming language, RBASIC, for custom tailored applications.

It offers many of the features found in information storage and retrieval systems plus the flexibility and other advantages generally associated with the generic DBMS. Revelation is a complex program with, as yet, few supporting materials. Setting up an application will not be as easy as with the typical Information Storage and Retrieval system or many DBMS. The new Advanced Revelation is somewhat easier to use than the original package.

SPECIAL PURPOSE SOFTWARE

Most special purpose packages have a narrower market and higher prices than general purpose packages. They are available from the software producer or their agents, and software support and maintenance is available from the producer. Since this kind of package (in particular, the information storage and retrieval packages) is more likely to be used for inhouse databases than the other types, we will describe selected packages in more detail.

Information Storage and Retrieval Software

The number of useful packages for textual applications has been growing in recent years. You will find a range of costs and capabilities to choose from and, unless your requirements are rather unusual, it is likely that you will be able to find one or more packages that will meet your needs.

An information storage and retrieval package (IS&R) is the best option for most textual databases for several reasons:

1. Even though prices may seem high, this will probably be the most cost effective approach because the database design steps are easily accomplished.
2. If the system has been available for some time, you will possibly be able to communicate with current users of the system. The producer should be willing to furnish you with references to some users. Calling or visiting these users can provide an opportunity to ask some probing questions and possibly allow you to try out the systems in a real situation. (You should recognize that the users may not be totally unbiased in their evaluation of their chosen system, but they will still be a valuable source.)
3. The cost will be known and the delivery date reasonably firm (unlike the option to program a system on your own).
4. Many vendors can provide a demonstration package, which you can use to test the system with a small amount of your own data. (Be aware that some systems show a fast response time with small databases and bog down with large ones; this is one reason for talking to current users.)
5. You can generally get a copy of the documentation for systems under consideration.
6. Reviews of many of the packages have been published.
7. These packages have been specifically written for this type of application. In particular they support variable length fields and records, repeating field/subfield values, and they offer powerful and flexible search capabilities.

The systems in this category are mainly of the single file type, in which all data values are stored in records in a main file. Retrieval is supported by relatively powerful query languages. Efficient retrieval is usually made possible in these systems through the use of inverted indexes. Other supporting files may also be used to support retrieval and overall system functions.

This *flat file* approach with inverted index is modeled after the large information retrieval systems such as DIALOG and BRS. Some data redundancy is generally present in these systems, though data compression techniques in some systems keep overhead to very acceptable levels. These systems are excellent for those applications where the database is fairly stable and where powerful search and retrieval capabilities are needed, but where capabilities for data manipulation on the retrieved data (such as numeric computations) is not required.

The report generation capabilities of these systems vary widely. Some, such as CAIRS, STAR, and INMAGIC, offer very powerful and flexible report generation; others such as Personal Librarian only display or print records in a fixed format.

Specific information storage and retrieval packages in this category are discussed in the following section. This is a selected list and we have no doubt left out some packages that are equally as worthy of mention. The packages are described in alphabetical order. Figure 7.1 summarizes some basic features of these packages.

BRS/SEARCH Micros/Mini Version. BRS/SEARCH Micros/ Mini Version is a derivative product of the BRS/SEARCH system developed and used on mainframe computers. It is a very powerful system offering extensive searching capabilities and is well suited for applications that involve processing of lengthy textual information. Very efficient storage allows for the indexing of every word with a low overhead ratio. BRS/SEARCH runs under the multi-user UNIX operating system, which runs on several high end microcomputers. It includes password security.

Search features include right, left, and internal truncation, word proximity, Boolean operators with unlimited nesting of parentheses, range searching and comparison searching, index browsing, and set building. Searches can be saved and executed on other files. The query language is very similar to the BRS online system, so users of the online system will feel comfortable with the micro version.

BRS/SEARCH micro version offers the possibility of upward migration to minicomputers or mainframes if the database grows beyond the capabilities of a microcomputer. As compared with most of the other packages discussed in this section, BRS/SEARCH is a large and complex system that requires a database administrator who is very familiar with the UNIX operating system, as well as having a knowledge of the BRS retrieval system.

Documentation includes two volumes: a User's Guide and a

System Administrator's Guide. A separate package, BRSMAINT, allows most of the maintenance functions to be performed through interaction with a system of menus, reducing the administrator's dependence on the guide.

CAIRS. CAIRS (Computer Assisted Information Retrieval System) was developed in 1972 for use on minicomputers and mainframes. It is now also available in three microcomputer versions (A, B, and C). Version C is the complete system, and A and B are subsets with fewer features. CAIRS is a very powerful system offering a great deal of flexibility in database design, indexing options, file security, and retrieval and output options. It too offers the possibility of upward migration to larger computers if the database outgrows the MS-DOS microcomputer it starts out on.

CAIRS offers a full range of search capabilities: Boolean combinations with parenthetical grouping of terms, truncation, range and comparison searching, set building, search save, index browsing, and sequential searching of unindexed fields.

Four modes of indexing are supported: automatic (word parsing), tagged (phrase parsing), full field, and manual keyword. The first three can apply to any field in the records, the last is applied to a special series of up to nine pages of additional space per record.

The thesaurus capabilities of CAIRS are particularly notable. The package includes a thesaurus building module. The online thesaurus can provide vocabulary control on input and search term expansion in queries. The thesaurus can act as a stop list, a go list, or can cause automatic replacement of an entered term with a preferred term.

The user interface is not easy to use. CAIRS is command driven, and the commands are cryptic codes rather than full descriptive words (e.g., SINV for Search Inverted Index and MFSF for Modify Field Synonym File). Extensive use of codes and special characters for all functions adds to the complexity. All of this taken together with a powerful but complex system makes CAIRS a relatively difficult system to learn. For those who need its extensive range of features, it may be worth the effort.

INMAGIC. INMAGIC has been available for use on minicomputers since 1980. Versions are now available for MS-DOS microcomputers. The package is powerful, flexible, and relatively easy to use. It offers flexibility in defining data structures, a powerful report generator, and a range of indexing options. Password protection is available on the field level.

Search features include nested Boolean queries, comparison and

FIGURE 7.1   Software Comparisons

Feature	BRS	CAIRS	INMAGIC	PRO-CITE	SCIMATE	PERSONAL LIBRARIAN	STAR
Operating system	UNIX	MS DOS	MS DOS	MS DOS	MS DOS	MS DOS	AMOS
Single/multi user	Multi	Both*	Both*	Single	Single	Single	Multi
User interface	command	command	command & menu	menu	menu	command	command & menu
Boolean	yes	yes	yes	yes	yes	yes	yes
Truncation	right, left, mid	right	right	right, left	right, left, mid	right	right
Comparison	yes	yes	yes	yes	no	yes	yes
Word proximity	yes	no	no	no	no	yes	yes
Browse indexes	yes	yes	yes	yes	no	yes	yes
Set building	yes	yes	yes	yes	no	yes	yes
Screen edit	yes	yes	yes	yes	yes	no	yes

Batch input	yes	yes	yes	yes	yes	yes	yes
Dynamic update	yes	no	yes	yes	yes	no	yes
Report generator	yes	yes	yes	yes	yes	no	yes
Max. # records	1M	64M	none	32,500	32,767		268M
Max. # fields	65,000	80	75	45	20	256	500
Max. size of field	255 sent. /para. 255 words /sent.	2000	none	16,000	1894	none	1.9MB
Max. size of record	paragraph	18,000	none	16,000	1894	none	1.9MB
Inverted index	yes	yes	yes	yes	option	yes	yes
Parsing	word, phrase	word, phrase, term, manual, combin.	word, term, both	word, phrase, author, title	word	word	word, phrase, both

*Multi user versions available at a higher cost

range searching, date searching, set building, right truncation, index browsing, and sequential scanning of nonindexed fields.

For each field INMAGIC offers the options of phrase parsing the first 60 characters of each subfield (term indexing), word parsing (keywords), or both. Up to 75 fields may be specified for each file and up to 50 fields may be indexed. Extensive indexing will generate a high overhead for index storage.

Interaction with INMAGIC is primarily via commands, but hitting the return key with no input will usually generate a menu screen that lists options. Also, each module includes a tutorial unit. Online help is available in Select (searching) mode.

The report generator module allows a great deal of control over output formats. This can be taken advantage of in adapting INMAGIC to a variety of library functions. A companion package, BiblioGuide: Using INMAGIC in Libraries, provides data structures and report formats ready-made for such applications as online catalogs, orders management, serials management, and loan management. Computational capabilities, such as addition, subtraction, multiplication, and division, are supported.

Sci-Mate. Sci-Mate has three parts: the Searcher, the Manager, and the Editor. The Searcher provides the capability of searching online systems and downloading, the Manager is the inhouse database component, and the Editor produces formatted bibliographies.

The Manager allows you to define up to 20 fields per record, and each record may contain up to 1,894 characters. For longer records Sci-Mate can link records and make them into one logical record.

For small files no indexes are created, rather a "map" file is created for each file. This is searched sequentially based on a fixed length "signature" for each record. (See the discussion of signature files in Chapter 3.) This approach offers reasonably fast response time for file sizes up to about 5,000 records, very low overhead, and dynamic updating. An inverted index option is available, which will speed searching with larger files.

Search features include Boolean logic, right and left truncation, and internal wild card characters. Parenthetical grouping of terms is supported only with the inverted file option, but that option does not support left-hand truncation. Other features such as set building, search save, comparison, or range searching are not possible with Sci-Mate. Retrieved records may be edited or deleted. No password security is included to prevent unauthorized changes.

A limited report generation function is included in the Manager (columnar reports only). The companion Editor module provides the capability of producing bibliographies formatted according to any of several standard styles (e.g., ANSI or University of Chicago Style Manual) as well as user defined formats.

Together, the three Sci-Mate modules provide a good personal information management system, which can be useful in institutional environments as well. It is easy to use, but the menu driven interface may seem a bit cumbersome after the system is learned.

Personal Librarian. Personal Librarian (formerly called SIRE) offers many novel and powerful searching capabilities not provided by other commercially available systems. The basis for the functioning of Personal Librarian is the generation of frequency counts for all significant word stems in the database and for each record.

Search features include the usual Boolean queries with parenthetical nesting, comparison operators, term adjacency, truncation, index browsing, and set building. In addition, Personal Librarian has many unique search features and user-friendly features. It allows natural language queries so users do not need to learn a search syntax. The initial system response to a query is a bar chart that shows the number of hits and their probable relevance based on the number of times the search words occur in each document. Records are displayed in rank order by word occurrence.

A term can be "expanded" to generate a list of additional terms that frequently co-occur with the expanded term. An expanded term may be used as a query component, which has the effect of searching the associated terms combined with OR logic. Additionally, a retrieved document may be used as a query component. This searches for other records that have words in common with the query document record.

File definition and record input must be done using an external word processor or other source of ASCII text. Personal Librarian does not include an input module. Each file can have up to 256 fields. If existing records in the database are modified, the entire file must be re-indexed.

Personal Librarian has powerful and unusual search capabilities. System maintenance, input, and report writing features, however, are not as well developed as are the searching features.

PRO-CITE. Pro-Cite is one component of the Searcher's Toolkit. The other components are Pro-Search, a front-end to BRS and DIALOG online systems, and Biblio-Links, a group of programs for converting records downloaded from BRS, DIALOG, OCLC, or RLIN into Pro-Cite format.

Pro-Cite offers data management functions of input, editing, and searching, together with bibliographic formatting according to several standard styles (e.g., ANSI, the Chicago Manual of Style, and others) as well as user defined formats.

Pro-Cite comes with 20 predefined work forms for 20 document types. In addition, the user can define six more work forms. A single file can use more than one work form, allowing document types such as books and journal articles to be easily mixed in a database. Records are variable length with up to 16,000 characters per record.

Search features of Pro-Cite include Boolean logic with parenthetical grouping of terms, left and right truncation, set building, date searching, field specific searching, comparison searching, and browsing. Pro-Cite can take a manuscript from an ASCII text file, select citations to include in the bibliography, and then format these according to a specified style.

Other functions offered by Pro-Cite include browsing or printing the index, eliminating duplicate records, sorting, and merging files.

Pro-Cite operates primarily with a menu interface and includes context sensitive help, making it a relatively easy system to use. It is available in both MS-DOS and Apple Macintosh versions.

STAR. Unlike the packages discussed so far, STAR is sold as a turnkey hardware and software system. STAR is a powerful, flexible, and easy to use database and information retrieval system. It allows users to define over 1,000 different databases, each of which can total over 250 million characters. Each record can contain up to 500 fields and fields may repeat. Each record can contain up to 32,000 lines (about 1.9 million characters). The system can be used for a wide variety of applications.

STAR offers Boolean operators with nested parentheses, truncation, numeric, alphabetic and date ranging, sorting, index browsing, search save features, and flexible formatting for online display or offline printing.

Interaction with the various modules is by means of full screen interfaces, which allow fill-in-the-blank responses. Commands are displayed at the bottom of the screen and can be invoked with a single letter. The Data Entry module includes options for data validation. Codes and abbreviations can be expanded automatically.

Library Automation Packages

Microcomputer software for the automation of the various functions in a library—cataloging, the online public access catalog (OPAC), circulation control, acquisitions, and serial control—is improving in quality and availability. Most of the packages that fall into this category are less flexible in terms of record definition and report writing, and offer more limited query capabilities. Many of the library automation packages integrate two or more of the previously mentioned functions. Generally these packages offer good security by means of passwords to gain access to functions that need to be controlled. If your application requires circulation control and/or acquisitions in addition to database building and searching, for example, you might find that one of the integrated library automation packages is your best choice.

Some available microcomputer packages that are designed for the typical library setting might be used for other types of inhouse databases also. The following packages are examples of what can be found in this category.

Mandarin. Mandarin is one of the more flexible of the microcomputer library automation packages in terms of record definition and report generation. Records may be defined with up to 221 fields; fields are variable in length up to 6,144 characters and can be repeatable. Groups of fields may repeat. Fields may be designated as indexed or not, and may be indexed either by term or key word.

Mandarin integrates the cataloging, OPAC, and circulation functions and includes a flexible report generator module. Inventory control is also supported.

Boolean searching is supported (AND, OR, NOT, and XOR), but parenthetical grouping of terms is not. Set building is supported, so complex queries can be performed in steps. Truncation and comparison searching are also supported. For novice users a menu driven interface leads the user through the process of formulating Boolean queries.

TINman, TINlib. TINman is a generic relational database management system, which handles variable length fields with no limits to field or record size. Records may have up to 64,000 fields, and fields may repeat with no limit. Multiple files can be linked with no limit. Single and networked multi-user configurations are available.

Search features include Boolean combinations with nesting, left- and right-hand truncation, proximity searching, set building, range searching, and browsing. The "navigation" search method is a form of browsing in which parts of a retrieved record are used as further queries.

A variety of specific applications are available based on TINman. TINlib is an integrated library automation package, which includes online catalog (OPAC), circulation, acquisitions, serials control, import and export of data, and management functions. A thesaurus management application is included in the basic TINman package, as well as a powerful report generator. Both run on IBM PC and compatibles.

Bibliography Software

Bibliography generation software is a category of special purpose software aimed at the specific task of generating properly formatted bibliographies. These packages generally include or are based on relatively powerful retrieval capabilities, but differ from the other packages in their specialized output formatting functions. Most allow a user to specify bibliographic formats, as well as including several standard styles, such as the University of Chicago Style Manual, ANSI, or Modern Language Association format. Many bibliography generators compare favorably with the IS&R packages for small textual database applications. They generally support variable length fields and records and offer flexible record definition capabilities. Representative examples are discussed briefly.

Sci-Mate Editor. The Sci-Mate Editor module works with the Sci-Mate Manager module. It produces formatted bibliographies using any of 15 style sheets supplied with the package or with user defined style sheets. Records may be entered with the Editor or transferred from the Manager. Bibliographies can be sorted in several ways, and citations can be merged with a manuscript for printing as footnotes.

Notebook II and Bibliography. Notebook II is a text oriented file manager designed for maintaining bibliographic files and printing bibliographies. Fields are variable length and can be between 20,000 to 50,000 characters long. Printed output can be formatted according to standard or custom formats. With the companion program, "Bibliography," the system can create bibliographies for word processing files.

Reference Manager. Reference Manager was designed for biomedical scientists who publish. It can be used to create bibliographic databases and can incorporate the references from the database into manuscripts for publication. Records may be entered from the keyboard or downloaded from online services using a companion program, Capture. An optional disk contains more than 100 common journal formats, primarily in the biomedical sciences.

Pro-Cite. The Pro-Cite module of the Searcher's Toolkit works with Pro-Search and BiblioLinks. It formats downloaded or keyboarded records according to any of several standard styles or by user defined styles. Pro-Cite will scan a manuscript for citations that are in its database and format them into a bibliography.

PROGRAMMING WITH A STANDARD LANGUAGE

This approach requires the greatest effort and entails the greatest risk of failure. It should be considered only if your requirements are so unusual that no other option fits and a programmer is available who understands textual database design. Development time and costs are likely to be much greater than with purchasing existing software. We mention this option for the sake of completeness, but it is not an option that makes sense for most people.

If you decide to program your system from scratch, the choice of programming languages is much better than it was just a few years ago. Programming environments and languages have improved considerably, in particular in the microcomputer arena. Operating systems such as UNIX and Pick in addition to MS-DOS and CP/M give the programmer a greater choice of productivity tools with which to work.

In addition to the old standards in programming languages (e.g., BASIC, FORTRAN, COBOL, PL/I), we now have C, Pascal, PROLOG, MODULA II, ADA, FORTH, and many others. Assembler languages have improved in recent years also, but many of the higher level languages compare rather favorably with assemblers in terms of efficiency. A small loss in run time speed is compensated for in faster program development and easier maintenance.

Languages differ significantly in the degree to which they facilitate database programming and text processing. While it is generally recognized that a skilled programmer can accomplish a task in any general purpose language, some make the job easier than others.

Features of a programming language to look for include powerful file handling capabilities (including support for random access files and variable length records), powerful string manipulation functions and procedures, long string variables, and functions and procedures with parameter passing.

FURTHER READINGS

Beiser, Karl. *Essential Guide to dBase III + in Libraries.* Westport, Conn.: Meckler Publishing Corporation, 1987. Programs and data files available on floppy disk from Meckler for an additional charge.

Daehn, R.M. "Methods and Software for Building Bibliographic Databases." *Canadian Library Journal* 42 (June 1985): 147–152.

Desposito, Joe. "File Managers Get a Face-Lift." *PC Magazine* (January 27, 1987): 119–133.

Ingebretsen, Dorothy L. "Information Management Software—A Selected Bibliography." *Database* 10 (December 1987): 27–34.

Leggate, Peter and Dyer, Hilary. "The Microcomputer in the Library: III: Information Retrieval from External and Internal Databases." *The Electronic Library* 4 (February 1986): 38–49.

Lundeen, Gerald and Tenopir, Carol. "Microcomputer-Based Library Catalog Software." *Microcomputers for Information Management* 1 (September 1984): 215–228.

Lundeen, Gerald and Tenopir, Carol. "Microcomputer Software for In-House Databases . . . Four Top Packages Under $2000." *Online* 9 (September 1985): 30–38.

Phillips, Brian. "Database Management Systems in Libraries: Beyond dBase II/III." *Library Software Review* 5 (March/April 1986): 62–66.

Pollard, Richard. "Microcomputer Database Management Systems for Bibliographic Data." *The Electronic Library* 4 (August 1986): 230–240.

Poor, Alfred. "Database Power Puts on an Easy Interface." *PC Magazine* (January 27, 1987): 109–117.

Tedd, Lucy A. "Software for Microcomputers in Libraries and Information Units." *The Electronic Library* 1 (January 1983): 31–48.

Tenopir, Carol and Lundeen, Gerald W. "Software Choices for In-House Databases." *Database* 11 (June 1988). In press.

Woods, Lawrence A. and Pope, Nolan F. *The Librarian's Guide to Microcomputer Technology and Applications.* Published for the American Society for Information Science. White Plains, N.Y.: Knowledge Industry Publications, 1983.

For additional readings on specific packages see the sources listed in Appendix D.

8

Software Evaluation

The growth in the number of software packages that can be used for inhouse databases has both negative and positive consequences for the inhouse database designer. On the positive side, there are so many packages to choose from that you are likely to find one that will be suitable for all but the most unusual needs. A potentially negative factor is the problem of keeping up with all of the new packages on the market and the changes in existing packages. Choosing from among so many can be confusing and time consuming. Thus, a systematic evaluation process is one of the most important steps in your database design.

FIRST STEP IN EVALUATION

Software evaluation is actually a multiple-step process. The first step is the feasibility study as described in Chapter 4. Without a feasibility study you cannot evaluate software because you will have no criteria by which to compare and evaluate the packages. The evaluation process allows you to select the package that most closely matches the needs and constraints of your situation. No one package will be best for every situation. The feasibility study provides an outline of the criteria by which to compare capabilities of various packages.

IDENTIFICATION OF SOFTWARE PACKAGES

The second step in software evaluation is to identify packages that may be of potential interest. Appendix B provides a list of selected software packages that are suitable for inhouse database creation. Chapter 7 discussed some features of several of these packages. Other sources that will aid in software identification include printed software directories, online software directory databases, review articles in library science and microcomputer magazines, knowledgeable colleagues, and professional conferences.

Appendix C is a list of selected printed and online software directories. The directories are of three main types: general microcomputer software directories, those that provide information on all software packages available for a particular computer or operating system, and those that include only database software or special library/information management software.

The online directories are similar to printed software directories, but are usually of the broader, comprehensive type. They include all types of software for a variety of computers and operating systems. An addition to the online directories is the PC-DBDB on floppy disk. PC-DBDB is an inhouse referral database that contains over 400 records describing information management software. It comes with the PC-File III software to search the database. Order information is included in Appendix C.

Neither the printed directories nor the software databases include substantive criticism of the various packages. In addition, they may not be updated frequently. You can use these directories to compile a preliminary list of software packages to be examined further. Directories typically include such information as hardware requirements, operating system required, price, and notable features.

Software reviews in the library and information science literature and in the microcomputer literature will help you to begin narrowing down your choices, as well as help you to identify new packages on the market. Several publicly available bibliographic databases will help you identify software reviews. *Microcomputer Index* (file 233 on DIALOG) and *Magazine Index* (on DIALOG, BRS, and NEXIS) index microcomputer and library literature and allow you to specify reviews. *Magazine Index* is also available on microfilm in many libraries, and *Microcomputer Index* is available as a printed index. The Computer Database (file 275) indexes evaluations and software comparisons of all types of products. Appendix D lists selected sources for locating software reviews. Magazines that are particularly good sources for reviews of inhouse database software are also listed in Appendix D.

Another source of information about software (and for candid reviews) is professional colleagues. Attendance at conferences, such as the American Society for Information Science annual meeting, Special Libraries Association annual conference, or International or National Online meetings, provides an opportunity to see new packages displayed in the exhibit hall and to talk informally with colleagues who have experience with the packages. Conference proceedings that regularly include information on textual database software are included in Appendix D.

Identifying software and reviews of software through directories, databases, articles, and meetings will leave you with a handful of packages that appear to be promising candidates for your inhouse database. You will then need to undertake an in-depth evaluation of these packages.

SOFTWARE EVALUATION FORM

Some sort of software evaluation form is a handy aid to ensure consistent and systematic evaluation of each package. Either of the forms shown in Figures 8.1 and 8.2 may be used or you may wish to design your own. You will undoubtedly want to add or delete certain criteria based on the information identified in your feasibility study.

Figure 8.1 (on pages 124–127) is a multi-page form that provides detailed analysis of all aspects of the software to be evaluated. Information that does not pertain to your situation can be crossed off or ignored. Examples of completed forms are given in Appendix A. These should be used as examples only because differing needs and priorities make it impossible to judge a software package in the same way for different applications.

As information is gathered about each package, the factual information as well as your comments and opinions for each software package are recorded on a separate copy of the form. When sufficient information is gathered about each package, a numerical comparison score can be assigned to each category on the form. For example, if one package has extremely good report generator capabilities, that package might receive a 5 (excellent) in that category. If, on the other hand, its search features are limited, the "searching" category might be rated 2 fair, or 1 poor. Packages that are unacceptable for your needs in any category are rated 0 for that section. Scores may be given to each individual item in each category or to the category as a whole. The overall score of any package is not a scientific number, but may be useful to serve as a cutoff point in narrowing down your choices to the few best packages. Of course, you may use the form without computing a numerical score.

The form shown in Figure 8.2 (on pages 128–129) is less detailed, but uses weighting of each item in each category to allow your individual needs to be more accurately reflected in the final overall

FIGURE 8.1   Software Evaluation Form

Name of package: _____ Version: _____
Producer: _____
Contact Person: _____ Phone Number:_____
Address: _____
★★
GENERAL CONSIDERATIONS:
Number of records supported: _____
Number of fields per record: _____
Restrictions on field lengths: _____
Variable length fields: _____
Multiple Values per field: _____
File Structures: _____
Overhead: _____
User designated Index fields: _____
DBMS or file manager: _____
Multiple user system: _____
Comments: _____

SCORE: +
              0   1   2   3   4   5
        (unacceptable)   (poor)   (fair)   (average)   (good)   (excellent)

HARDWARE REQUIREMENTS
Turnkey system: _____
Brand/model required: _____
Operating system(s): _____
Memory required: _____
Peripherals required: _____
Other peripherals supported: _____
Dedicated hardware required: _____
Comments: _____

SCORE: +
              0   1   2   3   4   5

DATA INPUT
Variety of input means: _____
Ease of input procedures: _____
New input identified: _____
User defined templates: _____
    Single or multiple templates per file: _____
Editing features: _____
    Screen editor or line editor: _____
    Global changes: _____

Ease of edit commands: _____
Updating (batch or dynamic): _____
Data verification: _____
Look-up tables: _____
Comments: _____

SCORE: +
      0   1   2   3   4   5

SEARCHING
Query language included: _____
Menu driven or command: _____
Ease of learning: _____
Error messages: _____
Set building: _____
Boolean operators: _____
Proximity searching: _____
Comparison or arithmetic operators: _____
Truncation: _____
Free text searching: _____
All fields searchable: _____
Individual fields searchable: _____
Save and rerun searches: _____
Vocabulary control: _____
Comments: _____

SCORE: +
      0   1   2   3   4   5

OUTPUT
Online screen display: _____
Report generator: _____
  User defined formats: _____
  System supplied formats: _____
  Ease of use: _____
Sorting: _____
  User defined: _____
  System supplied: _____
  Entire database or subset: _____
Arithmetic functions: _____
Comments: _____

SCORE: +
      0   1   2   3   4   5

FIGURE 8.1, Cont'd.

SECURITY
Passwords: _____
Security from alteration: _____
Dial-up access: _____
Log on procedure: _____
Usage tracking: _____
Back-up procedures: _____
Comments: _____
_____

SCORE: +
     0   1   2   3   4   5

TRAINING/DOCUMENTATION
Amount of training needed: _____
Online tutorials: _____
Different user levels: _____
Printed tutorials: _____
Training by vendor: _____
Documentation: _____
  Clarity: _____
  Comprehensiveness: _____
  Accuracy: _____
Other support materials: _____
Comments: _____
_____

SCORE: +
     0   1   2   3   4   5

VENDOR OR PRODUCER
Knowledge of textual databases: _____
Other products: _____
Years in business: _____
Reputation: _____
Date this product introduced: _____
Users of this product: _____
_____
Users' reactions: _____
Vendor accessibility: _____
Support services: _____
Your reactions: _____
Comments: _____
_____

SCORE: +
     0   1   2   3   4   5

OTHER CONSIDERATIONS
Cost: _____
Cost compared with similar programs: _____
Maintenance availability: _____
Upgrade procedures: _____
Lease/use restrictions: _____
Comments: _____

SCORE: +
       0   1   2   3   4   5

★★
SUMMARY SCORE: _____
FINAL COMMENTS: _____
_____
_____
_____
_____

score. Depending on how important each item is to your situation, weight values are assigned by you before software is examined. For levels of importance, in the first column, you would use a scale of one through ten: 0 = no importance, 5 = moderately important, 10 = very important, and * = essential. For the rating in column two you also use a scale of one through ten: 0 = not available, 3 = poor, 5 = acceptable, 8 = good, and 10 = excellent. To score you multiply the level of importance by the rating for each category and add all scores to determine the overall rating. If the software cannot provide a feature scaled as essential (*), then the software is disqualified.

As each software package is examined, a numerical score is assigned to each item. The overall score is computed by adding together all of the products for each item's weight times each item's score. Again this overall score is highly subjective and should not be considered as the only factor in software selection.

Software evaluation forms serve several purposes. They promote easier comparison among different packages by ensuring that all packages are judged by the same criteria. They serve as a memory jogger so that all the questions are answered for each package. They can be used as an interview schedule for discussions with vendors and users. Completed forms serve as handy summary sheets for each package. They can be used as an outline to expand your feasibility study into functional specifications. Finally, the software evaluation form forces you to write things down and to be evaluative on each point. This helps to ensure a consistent, systematic, and critical evaluation process.

FIGURE 8.2   Software Evaluation Form

Name of Software _____

Overall Rating _____

	LEVEL OF IMPORTANCE	RATING	SCORE
VENDOR/PRODUCER			
Reputation			
Library knowledge			
Other products			
Users of this product			
Response to this product			
Support services			
Geographic location			
Accessibility by phone			
Your reactions			
SYSTEM OUTPUT			
Display format			
Customizing features			
Printed lists			
Statistical reports			
Tape generation			
SYSTEM INPUT			
Special input			
Variety of input means			
Ease of procedures/commands			
Ident. of new input			
Ease of deletions, adds, changes			
Flexibility of format			
SEARCHING			
Query language			
User formats			
Error messages			
Thesaurus			
All fields searchable			
Distinction among fields			
Logical combinations			
Simple searching			
SECURITY			
Levels of passwords			
Security from alteration			

	LEVEL OF IMPORTANCE	RATING	SCORE
Log on procedures			
Back-up systems			
Usage tracking			
TRAINING			
Online training lessons			
Query language			
Documentation			
Training classes			
Ease of learning			
EQUIPMENT			
Hardware warranty			
Hardware reliability			
Trade-in benefits			
Downtime procedures			
Back-up procedures/features			
Service			
Ongoing costs			
Terminals			
Dial-up access			
Number of terminals			
Response time			
Other peripherals			
OTHER CONSIDERATIONS			
Size capabilities			
Clarity of costs			
Cost comparison with other systems			
Cost comparison with existing system			
TOTAL SCORE			

The form will only be part of the information you gather about each package. It is a good idea to keep a file or notebook about each package. This is the place to put vendor or producer literature, copies of criticism or reviews, your notes from informal discussions with users, and anything else of interest.

Filling Out the Form

The following discussion is based on the criteria listed on the Software Evaluation Form (Figure 8.1). Evaluation criteria can be separated into several major headings: general system characteristics or constraints, hardware requirements, data input features, searching features, output formats and flexibility, security, training and documentation, vendor or producer, and other considerations.

General System Characteristics or Constraints

The first things to record about a package are the general limitations or characteristics that will have important ramifications for your database. Any limitation on the total number of records supported by a package or the number of fields allowed per record should be discovered at the beginning of the evaluation process. (Of course, even if there are no size restrictions imposed by the software, there may be limitations imposed by the hardware.) Some packages identified early in the evaluation process may be eliminated if restrictions conflict with your feasibility study. Record and field limitations may sometimes be found in vendor literature, often in system documentation, but you may have to press the vendor for such information.

Any restrictions on length of fields should also be determined at the beginning of the evaluation process. Related to field length is whether a package allows variable length fields, or whether it uses fixed length fields. Fixed length fields are wasteful of computer storage, especially in textual databases where the same fields in different records tend to vary greatly. Since most textual databases require the capability of handling multiple values in a field, whether the software can accommodate multiple valued fields should be noted.

Determine the type of file structure used by each package. Inverted files will allow more search capabilities and efficiency, but use more computer space. This will usually be stated as the amount of overhead taken up by the programs, which will have a direct bearing on the number of records you can have in your database. If inverted indexes are supported, can the fields to be inverted be selected by the user? This will help to control the overhead. There may be restrictions on the number of fields that can be so designated.

Whether a package is a DBMS or file manager will be important if you want to support more than one interrelated file. It is also important to determine at the outset whether the system will support multiple users, if this is required in your situation.

The score rates this package in comparison with your needs analysis and with the other packages under consideration. A score of

0 (unacceptable) on the *general considerations* section of the evaluation form should eliminate this package from further consideration.

Hardware Requirements

The *hardware requirements* section continues general limitations and requirements. Much of the information in this section is
merely factual and may be found in literature from the vendor.

A turnkey system is one in which the hardware is sold with the
software. This means that your initial investment will probably be
greater, and the hardware cannot usually be used for other purposes.
On the other hand, a turnkey system is sure to have fully compatible
hardware and software and may relieve you of much of the worry of
hardware maintenance. If you purchase both hardware and software
for your database, you will have to make sure that the hardware
upkeep and warranty are covered in your purchase price.

Most software for microcomputer-based inhouse databases is
sold separately from the hardware. In these cases, note the hardware
required by the system. A majority of good textual database software
requires IBM-compatible microcomputers, often specifying a particular model such as XT or AT compatible. Such software usually
requires the MS-DOS or PC-DOS operating system, but may specify
another more sophisticated operating system, such as PICK or UNIX.

Internal computer memory required by the program will be
given in the vendor literature. External storage requirements will
vary with the size of your database.

Your feasibility study and subsequent data input decisions (see
Chapter 9) may have identified the need for certain peripheral
equipment. Examples of typical peripherals sometimes required for
inhouse databases include a modem, two floppy disk drives or a hard
disk drive, a dot-matrix printer, a CD-ROM player, an OCR scanner,
and a tape drive. Record what the program requires, plus any
limitations on what will be supported.

Data Input Features and Ease of Use

The Data Input section combines descriptive information with
evaluations. The question on variety of input means should be
answered with a list of the types of input supported by the package.
(See Chapter 9 for details of data input options.) Depending on project
requirements, any of several input options may be needed. If you will
be doing extensive retrospective conversion, for example, will the

system allow a tape generated by optical character recognition or other means to be used as input? If needed, can you download records from commercial databases to transfer to your database? If your needs analysis showed that your database would be relatively small and input would be done directly into the system, variety of input needs is not very important.

Ease of input, on the other hand, is important in every situation. It is a subjective judgment, based on the experience and skill of your input staff. As such, it is best determined by having your data entry personnel try the input procedures on a sample application of the software being evaluated. If the vendor will not send you a sample or review system and you know of no one who is using this software, reading the documentation is the next best way to get an idea of ease of input.

Does the system identify new input? This will help you to check the quality of work by your input staff and also allow current awareness profiles to be run whenever the database is updated.

Most software packages described in Chapter 7 allow the designer to select or create a template that defines the field structure and is used to prompt input. Some of the library applications packages, however, predefine the fields and order of input. When examining a package that has predefined templates, make sure that the structure fits your information needs. Most packages allow only one template per file, whether it is predefined or user designed. This may be a problem if your project has a variety of different record types.

Just as with input, editing features of every package examined should be tested if possible. If you cannot test a sample database, look very carefully at the description of methods for editing or input. Screen editors are almost always easier and more efficient to use and can save valuable time in a database that is updated frequently. Global change capabilities will allow you to keep the database up-to-date and enhance the change process. Edit commands should be easy to remember, preferably mnemonic.

How a program updates its inverted indexes will affect your update schedule. Some allow you to input all additions, corrections, and deletions into a word processing or editing program and then batch the updates at a time when the system is likely to be unused. Others update all indexes each time a change is entered (dynamic updating). In a large database this may cause undesirable delays. Some programs allow you to do either batch or dynamic updates.

Finally, under data input features, how much assistance does the software offer the data entry personnel? Packages vary in their capability to do verification on the data as it is input. Common verification procedures, such as checking a year field to make sure it is input as all numbers or checking the length of fields, help catch some erroneous input. Verification is probably of less help in bibliographic or full text databases that typically have varying field values than in directory or numeric databases that may have more predictable field values.

Assistance features that are uncommon in microcomputer software, but are useful in textual databases, are look-up tables that allow authority files or thesauri to be used online at input. If such a feature is available, it can provide valuable assistance in controlled vocabulary indexing.

Searching

Input features are important to the database maintenance personnel, but searching and output features are important to everyone. The power of the search features and ease of use will determine in most cases the success or failure of your database. Search features must be evaluated with the needs and experience levels of your users in mind at all times.

Does the program include a query language, or must you program it yourself? Information storage and retrieval packages almost always have powerful query languages, but a general purpose DBMS may not. If there is a query language, is the interface to it menu driven, command driven, or can the user choose? The experience of your users and frequency of their use of this database will determine which is best for your needs. Whether it is menu or command driven, how easy is it to learn to use the system? Learning time will vary from nearly instantaneous to many hours of required training.

Related to ease of use is the efficacy and meaning of error messages. Error messages should be clear and provide diagnostic information rather than just tell a user that a command was incorrect. The best way to test error messages is to purposely make errors when searching a sample database that uses the software being evaluated. Often error messages are listed in the software manuals, but it is difficult to judge their utility out of the context of a particular error. If no or few error messages are supplied with the software, can the database designer easily add others to the system?

It is important to compare the search features of the various software packages because they vary so much and because search power is likely to be the most important part of your database. Record whether or not a package offers a feature such as set building or Boolean logic *and* any limitations or special power of those features. (For example, some packages only support the Boolean AND and OR operators with no nested logic.) Any extra search features can be recorded in the comments section. If vocabulary control features such as look-up tables for vocabulary switching can be invoked in searching, these features should be recorded here also.

Output

Searching features will in some ways determine the output possible from your database, but there are other features that address output capabilities directly. First, examine the online screen displays that result from a search. Can they be customized or is there just one standard screen display? Is the display clear, uncluttered, and appropriate for your users?

What kind of printed reports can be generated? Some packages allow only printing of the screen image, others allow you to choose from among or define a variety of output formats. What are these capabilities and how easy are they to invoke? Can printed reports be made of the entire database (e.g., a book catalog), of subsets of the database only, or of both? Can these reports be sorted by specified criteria? How much control do you have over the sorting?

Finally, regarding output, does the software allow any statistical reports to be generated? For example, can you do arithmetic calculations on specified fields or can you get management reports about the number of records or characters in the database? The need for such reports will of course be dependent on your particular situation.

Security

Security in terms of users and backup procedures should also be evaluated. If you need to have password access, is it available and at what levels? Can you specify some users as searchers only, while others have the capability to change the contents of records? Is dial-up access supported, and if so, what security precautions are included? Is the log on procedure simple enough so it does not inhibit use, but complex enough that unwanted users cannot easily get on?

You may want to track the use of your database in terms of passwords used and queries submitted for security purposes and for purposes of evaluation and improvement of the database. Is such usage tracking supported and to what degree?

Finally, under security, what are the system backup procedures? Are backups of new information automatically made or must a backup be initiated by the database maintenance personnel? How frequently are backups made? Are special backup peripherals (e.g., a videotape machine) required or supported?

Training/Documentation

How much training is needed before someone can search, input, or generate reports on the system? Is this training supported online through tutorials or different levels of query languages and help commands? Are printed tutorials available, and if so, are they necessary before use? Is training of users or data entry personnel supplied by the software vendor and is it required before use?

Examine all documentation carefully. You may be able to purchase user manuals separately from the software when you are doing your evaluation process. This is recommended if you cannot obtain the documentation elsewhere, because it is essential to examine documentation to know what you are getting. Have several people look at printed manuals to judge clarity and comprehensiveness. If you have access to the software, you may also be able to judge accuracy of the documentation and other support materials.

Vendor or Producer

The vendor and producer of a program may or may not be the same. (For general purpose software they are likely to be different, while for special purpose packages they are often the same.) You need to evaluate both the vendor and the producer.

Although much of this evaluation is based on your subjective impressions of the companies and individuals you will be dealing with, it is important nonetheless. Even if the purchase price of a package is relatively inexpensive, you will have a substantial investment in a database once you have designed it and input records. For those reasons you want to feel comfortable about the reputation, responsiveness, and quality of the companies who have written and/ or sell the software.

Their knowledge of textual databases, quality and scope of other products (if any), and track record in the software business will all tell you something about the stability and knowledge of the vendor and producer. Find out also if there are any users of this product who have needs and records similar to your project. Contact these users if possible.

The accessibility and support offered by software vendors will vary considerably. General purpose software vendors can be expected to be less involved with an individual customer's applications. Does the vendor offer needed extra support services, such as data conversion or implementation of the software on your hardware? Is the vendor accessible to answer questions by phone if not in person? This level of service may be provided free by the vendor or for a fee. Generally speaking, the more generalized a microcomputer package is, the fewer the special services that will be offered.

Other Considerations

The last section of the software evaluation form is a summary of other considerations, notably cost and lease or purchase requirements. Most of this information should be readily available from the vendor. Although cost is a practical limitation, it should not be the overriding evaluation criterion. For inhouse database applications, the software packages that have done the most work for you generally have the highest prices. Therefore, your time and customizing costs may be considerably higher for some seemingly bargain-priced packages.

GATHERING THE INFORMATION

Your strategy for gathering all of this information will include a variety of tactics. The first step should be to contact, in writing, each of the producers of packages you will be evaluating in depth. Contacting the producer directly will ensure that you have information about the latest version of the software, something that might not happen if you begin your evaluation with printed reviews or advertisements in the literature. In your letter, you might include parts of your needs analysis or rewrite the analysis in the form of a list of questions. Since most software for inhouse microcomputer-based databases costs in the range of only $100 to $2,500, formal functional specifications submitted to producers in the form of a Request for Proposal (RFP) are usually not used. It would simply not be worth the time and cost for most of these producers to respond to such a detailed RFP. (This would be the procedure for larger systems with greater software expenditures.) Ask the producer to include the name of a local vendor or distributor of the company's package, and, for information retrieval packages, names and addresses of users.

Not all producers will respond to your request. The larger producers of general purpose DBMS deal in such a large volume of sales that they may respond with only a copy of the latest advertising brochure. If this is the case, send your request to the local vendor or distributor.

When you receive a written reply you can begin to fill out the factual portions of your evaluation. Undoubtedly some of the factual questions will still be unanswered. This is a good time to contact the producer or distributor by telephone. You can ask for more detailed information, plus you can get a feel for the responsiveness of the company. This will let you begin to answer the subjective questions in the Vendor/Producer section of the software evaluation form.

Your next step (often done while you are waiting for replies to your letters) is to locate reviews and opinions about each package. Sources for locating published software reviews have already been mentioned and are listed in Appendix D. It is a good idea to keep copies of reviews in your software file or notebook to refer to again. Next, contact users of the package if you can. People are likely to be more candid on the telephone or in person than they will be in a letter. Call or visit if at all possible. Try to see the software in action. The best way to judge ease of use and capabilities is to sit down and work with an actual database. Try to find users who will let you view and work with their databases. If this is not possible, at least have the producer send a demonstration version of the software for you to try, or have the vendor come to your location for a hands-on demonstration. There is no substitute for seeing the package in action.

The database applications you examine should be as similar to your situation as possible. This may be difficult to find for the general purpose DBMS or file manager packages. Remember that the unique characteristics of textual databases impose unique requirements on a package, and you should judge a package on how well it responds with that type of database. Just because a package is working fine for an inventory or name/address file application does not mean it will perform for your more complex database. It is best to locate users of general purpose packages through descriptions of their projects that they have written in the professional literature.

You will also want to examine the documentation of a package. If you cannot visit an installation, there is no local distributor, and the producer is unwilling to send a test copy of the software, purchasing the documentation may be the only way you can judge the software capabilities and ease of use. If a producer will not lend documentation to you for examination purposes, you may wish to purchase it. For packages seriously under consideration this is probably worth the cost. Remember your investment in your database goes far beyond the purchase price of the software.

FURTHER READINGS

Balaban, Donald J.; Wright, Gail K.; Innes, Frank and Goldfarb, Neil. "Choosing a Micro Database for Easy Retrieval of Reprints," *Clinical Computing* 4 (no. 3, 1987): 23–29.

Beiser, Karl. "Database Management Software: A Selection Guide." *Wilson Library Bulletin* (June 1986): 17–19.

Garoogian, Rhoda, "Pre-written Software: Identification, Evaluation, and Selection," *Software Review* 1 (February 1982): 11–34.

Kazlauskas, Edward John. "Information Management Software Guidelines for Decision Making." *Database* 10 (December 1987): 17–25.

Kelley, David. "Software—What's Available?" In Ching-chih Chen and Stacey E. Bressler, eds. *Microcomputers in Libraries*, 65–74. New York: Neal-Schuman, 1982.

Look, Hugh E. "Evaluating Software for Microcomputers." *The Electronic Library* 2 (January 1984): 53–60.

Oliver, K.B. "Methodology for Selecting Software for an Online Database." In *Proceedings of the 9th International Online Information Meeting*, 461–465. Medford, N.J.: Learned Information, 1985.

Tenopir, Carol. "Evaluation of Library Retrieval Software." In *Communicating Information: Proceedings of the 43rd Annual Meeting of the American Society for Information Science*, v. 17, 64–67. Allen R. Benenfeld and Edward John Kazlauskas, eds. White Plains, N.Y.: Knowledge Industry Publications, 1980.

Tenopir, Carol. "Identification and Evaluation of Software for Microcomputer-Based In-House Databases," *Information Technology and Libraries* 3 (March 1984): 21–34.

Tenopir, Carol. "In-House Databases II: Evaluation and Choosing Software." *Library Journal* 108 (May 1, 1983): 885–888.

9

Building and Maintaining the Database

Once your database is designed and the software installed, there remains the not insignificant task of getting the information into the database. This can be the most costly and time-consuming part of the entire process. In addition to retrospective conversion there are ongoing procedures for continued input and database maintenance. This chapter discusses the procedures needed to build and maintain your database, including conversion options, input procedures, back-up policies, and policies to ensure quality control.

PREPARING FOR CONVERSION

It is very likely that a collection of items exists to which your database provides access. The task of record conversion assumes that there also exists some type of file to convert. This is not always the case. The person implementing the database may be presented with a room full of books in boxes, or reprints in file cabinets or in piles on the floor, or a slide collection with no current organization.

Whatever the state of the collection and its current access mechanism or lack thereof, this would be a good time to consider weeding the collection. The conversion process will require time, money, and machine storage, so it is preferable not to convert unnecessary items.

One approach to converting a library collection is to convert items as they are returned from use (assuming that the current system can function parallel to the new system as the conversion progresses). The 80/20 rule very likely will apply, meaning that 20 percent of the items in the collection will account for 80 percent of the use. By converting items as they are returned from use, the active 20 percent will be converted first. The remaining 80 percent can be converted later as time permits or as these items are eventually used. Items not used after some period of time may be considered prime candidates for weeding.

Deciding what and how much to convert initially may be made on criteria other than use. Establishing conversion cut-off points (such as not converting documents published before a certain date) are clear-cut if somewhat arbitrary. If there is a natural division in your collection, the conversion decision may be easier. Converting only those items housed in one of multiple locations or only journal articles or books in a multi-format collection may be logical decisions. Setting priorities for conversion will help the database maintenance staff plan their budget, time, and hardware resources.

Future use of the database should be considered when planning for conversion. If only abbreviated bibliographic records are needed now, is there is a future need for more complete records? If so it will probably pay to convert to full records now in order to avoid having to repeat the conversion process at some future time. On the other hand, if full text is not required now but will be in the future, it probably will not pay to convert complete texts until needed. These decisions, of course, affect the amount of computer storage space required now and in the future.

UPDATING

Many of the decisions for data entry are the same whether you are retrospectively converting a large number of records or updating the database on a continuing basis. The following discussion applies to both, except where a difference is noted.

The process of updating includes adding new records to the database, correcting errors in old records, and deleting records that are duplicated or no longer of use. Update procedures will depend in part on software capabilities and in part on scheduling factors, such as the work schedule of the data entry personnel and the amount of time the database system is in use.

Different software packages handle updates in different ways. In small databases that generate no inverted indexes, it can be a simple matter to add, delete, or change a record. The new material is merely added on to the linear file. When a software package creates inverted indexes, as is common in most information storage and retrieval programs, there is another step in the updating process. After records are input or corrected, the program must parse each designated field in each record and merge them into the existing inverted indexes. This can be a time-consuming process, that varies with the software package and specifications you have set up for each field.

Updating modes offered by software are dynamic, batch, or a choice of either. The best procedure for updating will vary according to how many additions, corrections, or deletions must be made. If there is a relatively small volume, new input can be added dynamically on an as-needed basis. After each record is input, the system will completely update the inverted indexes. In a small database with a small number of updates this wait will probably not be too long.

Batch updates may be desirable if your collection is growing rapidly or when many records are being retrospectively converted for input. For locally created records, a word processor is typically used to create the batch update file. Any word processing package that creates standard ASCII files will work. The database system is thus available for users while the keying-in is taking place. Because the computer is tied up while the indexes are being updated, it is often desirable to do inputting on a regular schedule. Users and staff alike can thus predict when the system will be available for use. Batched records can be input during regular work hours, and the inverted indexes can be regenerated overnight.

CONVERSION OPTIONS

There are two main options for getting records into your database. The first is to create the records specifically for your database; the second is to use existing machine readable records. Several ways to accomplish each of these options are discussed in this section.

Key to Disk

Direct keyboard entry of new records is generally the most costly option, but often is the only viable one. Many inhouse databases contain information of local origin that is not available in published machine readable form. For example, an engineering firm may have a collection of engineering drawings that it wants to provide access to, or a pharmaceutical firm may need to provide access to its laboratory notebooks, or an individual may want to organize his photo collection. In each of these examples, and many other situations like them, there is no choice but to key in the data. Key to disk is probably the most common mode of keyboard input. This involves storage on magnetic disk of data entered via the keyboard. Key to disk entry is done either by interacting with the database software or by using a separate word processing package for subsequent batch loading into the database.

Database Software. The input modules that come with database software vary in terms of power and ease of use. Input features was one criterion by which you evaluated your software package (see Chapter 8). When using the database software to input records, the following features are desirable:

- screen oriented (rather than line oriented) input and editing
- commands and function keys that are easy to remember (preferably mnemonic)
- the ability to carry over values from one record to the next when the same values are required in more than one record
- the ability to provide default values automatically where appropriate (e.g., the local city and state in the address fields of personnel records)
- the use of coding tables to allow expansion of short input into fuller forms (an example would be a table of zip codes that would automatically expand to city and state when the zip code is entered)
- data validation features such as format and range checks
- the ability to verify values in selected fields by authority files or thesauri
- the ability to make global changes
- the choice of batch or dynamic updating

Word Processing Software. Some database software packages have poor data entry modules or none at all. Simple data entry features may be sufficient for occasional additions or changes, but impractical for large-scale retrospective conversion. In all of these cases, a separate word processing software package may be a better (or necessary) option for key to disk entry.

Any word processing package that creates standard ASCII files will work. It is best to use a package that has the edit features noted above. Your data entry personnel will feel most comfortable with a word processing package that they use in their daily work.

Contracting out. If you will need to retrospectively convert many thousands of records, you may want to contract out the keying work to a firm that specializes in this. Firms such as Saztec, Inforonics, Access Innovations, Inc., and others take print copies of your data and convert them to the specified machine readable format. The conversion is done frequently in locations outside of the country to keep the costs down.

OCR

Optical character recognition (OCR) offers another way to convert data. Before the widespread availability of microcomputers, information was often typed with a special OCR typeface on an IBM Selectric typewriter. This information was then read into an OCR scanning machine for conversion to a magnetic tape.

OCR technology has progressed to the point that it offers some help in converting material originally typed for some other purpose (letters or memos, for example). Inexpensive desktop OCR scanners are now on the market. Unfortunately, OCR technology has not progressed to the point where a librarian can dump card catalog drawer contents into a hopper or feed all the books and journals in a collection into an OCR machine and have the data automatically converted. Standard 8½-by-11-inch typed documents can be handled reasonably well, but bound books and journals, 3-by-5-inch cards, and other sizes and formats are not accommodated very well. OCR scanners do not deal well with varying typefaces or complex page layout. In addition to the conversion of each printed or typed character to its machine-readable code, there is the task of recognizing field, subfield, and record boundaries. This is a difficult task if the data was not originally organized with the conversion in mind.

The Kurzweil Data Entry Machine can convert nonstandard text to machine-readable form. It offers some hope, but it is still too expensive for most small projects and has an error rate such that the converted information needs to be proofread. Continuing improvements with OCR scanning, however, does offer promise for the future.

Data Entry Form

The data entry process will be made easier and more reliable if a data entry form (or worksheet) is used. This puts the data to be entered in an organized sequence and provides guidance as to form of entry, record contents, and so on. The fields on the data entry form should match the sequence in which the data will actually be entered. Figure 9.1 shows a typical data entry form.

Converting Machine-Readable Data

Data already in machine-readable form may be available if your inhouse database consists of published material such as article reprints or books. Data for these types of materials are available in

FIGURE 9.1 Data Entry Form

SUBJECTS	SUBDIVISIONS (if needed)
1) _____	_____
2) _____	_____
3) _____	_____
4) _____	_____
5) _____	_____
6) _____	_____
7) _____	_____
8) _____	_____
9) _____	_____
10) _____	Obituary _____

AUTHOR(S)
1) _____
2) _____

TITLE (with annotation): _____
_____
_____
_____

MONTH: January   April   July   October   DATE: _____
        February   May   August   November
        March   June   September   December   YEAR: _____

PAGE: _____   COLUMN: _____   COLUMN INCHES: ___
Illustration ☐   Editorial ☐   Letter ☐

NEWSPAPER: Hawaii Tribune Herald   Honolulu Advertiser
            West Hawaii Today   Honolulu Star-Bulletin

	Initials/Date
Student:	_____
Indexer:	_____

several forms: online from database services or bibliographic utilities, on magnetic tape from the utilities or from the Library of Congress, or on floppy disks or CD ROM from some database producers.

Existing Data

Locally generated data may already be in machine-readable

form. For example, word processing files might constitute the database, or there may already exist a database system that is being replaced by a new system. In this case the data may require reformatting before being loaded. Most word processing programs and database programs offer an option to write data to an ASCII file, and most database software is capable of importing data from ASCII files. Some direct package to package transfers are possible without conversion to ASCII format as an intermediate step. This depends on the two programs involved (one can, for example, transfer data for dBASE III to R:BASE System V and vice versa, or from Lotus 1,2,3 files to dBASE III). Information storage and retrieval software generally requires conversion to ASCII before input.

Downloading. Downloading of selected records from online vendors can be a convenient way to build a local database. Copyright considerations will vary, so anyone planning to use this approach should check with the database producer first.

Downloading involves the use of a microcomputer with communications software that supports the transfer of ASCII data from a host computer to a disk file on the local microcomputer. Most microcomputer communications software will do this. The data received by the microcomputer are held in an area of the computer's memory set aside by the communications software as a buffer. The user can open and close the buffer to begin and end data capture. When data transfer is complete the contents of the buffer are written to a disk file. The buffer may not be large enough to hold large amounts of data. When the buffer gets full its contents are automatically written to disk, and the buffer is reused for the next installment. This process of writing to the disk may take a few seconds, during which time the data capture process is interrupted. In order not to lose data the communications software will signal the host computer to stop sending, then when the buffer has been written to disk the software signals the host to resume sending. (This signaling usually uses a protocol known as X-ON, X-OFF, which uses a control-S to signal stop and control-Q to start.) The host computer must recognize the stop and start signals and act accordingly. Not all host systems are programmed to do this, but for those that are not, the value-added networks can be instructed during the log on process to handle the interruptions.

The data transferred by downloading will be in an ASCII (or text) file, which can be processed locally with a word processor or other special purpose software. In transferring records from an online database to your local database the local database software will need to be able to recognize individual records and fields. If the downloaded records have field tags, then some inhouse database software will be able to automatically incorporate them into the local database. If there are no field tags, then the records will require additional human analysis to indicate what constitutes fields and records. Some software helps with this process (e.g., Sci-Mate); for other software you will have to use a word processor to add field tags and reformat.

Since the data are available online, there must be some particular reason for wanting them stored in a local database as well. It may be that usage is high enough so that the savings in online charges will justify their inclusions in the local database or perhaps the data will be modified for local use. Downloading is the option selected by the case study in Appendix A.

Several of the software packages mentioned in Chapter 7 include the facility to transfer records from online databases (e.g., the Pro-Search and BiblioLinks packages that work with Pro-Cite of the Searcher's Toolkit, Notebook II with Convert, Sci-Mate, and Reference Manager). Costs associated with this approach include online database access charges, telecommunication charges, and often, per record type or display charges. Often the same data can be accessed through more than one online vendor at different costs. For example, the "after hours" services offered by BRS and DIALOG are less costly than their regular services, but provide access to fewer databases.

Magnetic Tape

Library utilities (OCLC, RLIN, UTLAS, and WLN) can provide bibliographic records through online capture or by means of magnetic tapes containing selected records. This type of service is limited to libraries that subscribe to the services. The microcomputer database project is generally operating on a different scale. Single library membership will be costly. Costs can be reduced somewhat by joining a consortium or local network that has access to one of these services.

Similarly, the Library of Congress offers tape service whereby libraries can send lists of LC card numbers in machine readable form and have the Library of Congress match these against its database to produce a tape with full MARC records (Machine Readable Cataloging). Most microcomputer systems are not configured to handle nine track tape and will need to have the records copied to floppy disks.

MARC is a standard format for recording bibliographic information in machine-readable form for communication from one computer to another. The MARC format accommodates variable length fields and subfields, employing numeric tags and special character sequences to mark the beginnings and ends of each logical unit. It is widely used by libraries for transferring bibliographic records. The data in the MARC record is often reformatted for processing by local software.

Commercial firms will also perform this kind of service. Notable is Carrollton Press with its REMARC project. It offers pre-MARC records going back to 1879. The REMARC database is also available through the DIALOG service.

Conversion approaches that are based on access to MARC record databases presume that the software being used for the local database accepts MARC records, or (more likely) includes a module that will convert from MARC to the internal format used by the system. Not surprisingly the library automation software is the category that generally supports this approach. The other categories discussed in Chapter 7 generally do not.

Floppy and CD ROM Disks

Some producers of publicly available databases are now offering subsets of their databases on floppy disks. Some are offering subsets or entire databases on CD ROM.

The Bibliofile system is specifically designed and marketed as a means of creating local databases from MARC records. In this system a set of four CD ROM disks hold approximately 3 million post-1965 MARC records. These disks are searched by any of several retrieval keys, and the retrieved records copied to floppy disk. Records may be edited, for example, to add local holdings information. The system will also produce card sets and book labels. This approach offers a fixed cost with unlimited use of the database. The makeup of the collection to be converted will determine if this would be a viable approach. If most of the items are pre-1965 or are not books, then this would not be very useful.

CD ROM is also being used to distribute bibliographic databases containing records for nonbook materials. Several firms are marketing CD ROM packages with search software for databases such as ERIC, Dissertations Abstracts, Agricola, Medline, Psychological Abstracts, and many others. These systems are intended to be used as the basis for local searching with a CD ROM player attached to the microcomputer, not as a source of records to be transferred to a magnetic disk file, though this may be technically feasible. Again, copyright considerations may arise. If the coverage is appropriate, this may substitute for the creation of a local database.

Another way that database producers have distributed database subsets is on floppy disks. ERIC Microsearch and BIOSIS BITS are examples of this approach. These are distributed with retrieval software, but could be used with other software as well. BIOSIS BITS service offers predefined subsets or custom subsets to match specific needs.

The creation of a CD ROM disk with local database records is a possibility also. If there is need for multiple copies of the database and if the database is large and not volatile, this may be an option to consider. For example, Group L Corporation markets a retrieval product, DELVE, and CD ROM mastering service to create large inhouse full text or bibliographic databases.

BACKUP PROCEDURES

Hardware approaches to backup are discussed in Chapter 2. To ensure continued maintenance of the inhouse database, the database administrator must choose from among the various hardware options and set a policy for timely backup procedures. If batch input is used for file updates, copies of the batch files should be kept as a form of backup. They can be used to reconstruct the database or parts of it if something is lost. The entire database should be periodically backed up as well, including index files. Ideally the entire database should be backed up after each modification or update to the database.

The magnetic media used for the backup can be recycled, but it is recommended that you keep at least two generations of the backup (e.g., the most recent copy and the one previous to that). When the next backup is made this frees the older copy for reuse. It is recommended that two backup copies be made, one kept onsite for convenience and one kept offsite for extra security, perhaps in a fireproof vault but at least in another building. Alternatively, store your second generation backup copy offsite together with copies of your latest batch update files.

Facilities for backing up the database will vary among the various database software packages. This is a feature to look for in your software evaluation. Separate software packages are available to handle the backup process, as well, and the operating system offers some facilities for backup.

Having a spare copy of locally produced documentation kept in a safe place is a good idea also. Transaction files recording all changes to the database should be kept. Some software will automatically generate transaction logs, with others you will have to keep records independently. If the transaction logs are kept in a file, you might want to print hard copies or make backup magnetic copies of these also.

Magnetic disks, tapes, and photocopies are cheap in comparison to the cost, time, and effort that will have been put into your database. It should be pointed out that magnetic media degrade with time, so tapes should be copied every two years if they are not superseded by newer backup copies.

QUALITY CONTROL

Maintaining a high quality database requires time and effort. Errors in your database will not only look bad, they may have a direct effect on retrieval. Database quality is determined by several things, including careful data gathering procedures, consistent use of each field, care in creation of value-added fields such as subject descriptors, error checking (verification) at input, and ongoing proofreading and provision for corrections.

Data Gathering

In a bibliographic database that provides retrieval to an existing physical collection, the data gathering stage is straightforward. Values for each field are entered to create records that describe each physical item in the collection. Other than weeding and priority decisions there is no need to decide what data goes into the system. Not all data gathering is so simple, however.

A bibliographic database that does not correspond directly to a physical collection, but instead attempts to provide bibliographic control over a given literature, encounters more difficulties at the data gathering stage. As described in Chapter 5, the initial editorial policies regarding information to be included in a database are frequently prone to unrecognized biases. Inadvertently leaving out literature from a certain region or of a particular type, for example, can directly affect the overall quality of your product. A searcher might approach a database with the idea that it provides comprehensive retrieval of information on a particular topic. If she or he misses relevant information because it is not included in the database, the quality of the research may suffer. The database designer has an obligation to users to gather source materials in a systematic fashion with well-documented exclusion and inclusion policies.

Ongoing care in gathering source materials may be even more important in a full text or referral database. Users of a business referral database, for example, need to feel confident that names, addresses, and descriptions of companies are up-to-date and accurate. Compiling this information with care and verifying its accuracy are obligations recognized by the quality conscious database creator.

Solutions to data gathering quality problems are not easy. Clear inclusion criteria and the publication of a list of sources are aids for a bibliographic database. Well thought-out and clearly documented data gathering procedures are helpful for all types of databases. Assigning data gathering tasks to qualified and well trained personnel, with cross checks by other personnel, is probably the best insurance against data gathering errors. Accuracy cross checks can be done by another staff member within the unit that is creating the database, by a qualified and conscientious user or group of users, by an outside agency such as an information broker hired on a part-time basis, or by verifying referral database contents with representatives of the organizations referred to in the database.

Continuous monitoring procedures to discover and correct outdated information need to be undertaken with the same care as initial data gathering procedures.

Consistent Use of Fields

It is simple to control quality issues that arise after data are gathered. Many of these issues can be controlled by accurate documentation and adequate training of all levels of personnel (see Chapter 10). Ensuring consistent use of fields relies on good field specification in the early stages of the database design (see Chapter 6). By planning carefully what fields are needed to describe any type of record, the database designer attempts to address future quality control. A carefully documented data dictionary that includes a definition of each field and data element, a description of its characteristics, and rules for formatting input with examples helps to ensure consistency.

Unfortunately, most microcomputer software does not help much with ensuring consistent field use. Microcomputer software typically allows only one record type per file. If your file includes several types of records (articles, books, engineering drawings, and slides, for example), one master record template has to be created to serve all types. This master template lists all of the fields that may be used in any record type. A master record template puts a burden on the data entry personnel and may be confusing. It requires the data entry person to select all of the fields and only those fields that are appropriate for a given type of document. It limits the options for automatic data validation.

Quality of Value-Added Indexing

Procedures for indexing are discussed in Chapter 5. Quality control begins with the initial decisions regarding use of some sort of controlled vocabulary. Use of a thesaurus aids quality by providing assistance in selecting the correct level of terms, as well as controlling word forms and formats. Formulation of logical and clear rules for indexing contributes significantly to quality control. All such policies should be documented.

Choosing well trained indexers, who are also subject experts, should improve the quality of indexing. Frequently, however, small inhouse databases cannot afford the luxury of a skilled indexer. A secretary may do the job, or users may be asked to select terms. Having only one person do the indexing or verify the index terms selected by users may at least increase consistency.

Ongoing quality control of a subject descriptor field can be helped by having a second person verify or spot-check terms. Any double-checking has to be approached with reason, however, because there are bound to be personal differences in choice of index terms. No vocabulary ensures absolute consistency because several approaches to indexing may be equally valid. Another reason for caution is that too much double-checking with concern over absolute accuracy is bound to create intolerable time lags. In most cases, providing reasonably accurate retrieval points quickly is more valuable than perfect indexing.

Error Checking at Input

Some error checking at input relies on the data entry personnel; some can be handled by the computer software. If the data entry staff uses a well-designed worksheet (see Figure 9.1) that corresponds to the system input screens, all they have to do at input is transcribe the information. Such a worksheet separates the input function from the intellectual analysis function. Although it might mean a slight delay of input, fewer input errors probably result.

Some labor-intensive options for input error detection include printing a list of all new input and manually proofreading, inputting all new information twice, having the computer compare the two versions, displaying or printing out any discrepancies, or printing out the inverted index to proof for typographical or format errors.

Most software can use parts of your data dictionary to do some automatic validation at input. Numeric fields, for example, should only accept numeric values. Date type fields should be numbers of a specified length. Fixed length fields should not have more or fewer characters. The system should disallow any values that do not meet these criteria, reminding the data entry person of valid parameters.

Simple validation is available on almost every package. Some packages will also match new input with the values already existing in the inverted index. If new values are input, the system will ask for verification. This helps catch typographical errors, and, as the database grows, will create an ad hoc authority file.

Automatic matching of a separate controlled vocabulary file is not usually available with microcomputer systems. Ideally, the software should be able to take each term entered in each field, determine from the data dictionary if there are any rules for the field or any authority control files, match input values with those listed in the authority file, change input from any unused term (SEE reference) to an acceptable term, and tell the data entry person if there is no term match. The reality is that in many cases this entire process must be done by the data entry personnel.

If batch input is supported by a package, the powers of a word processing program can be used for quality control. Many word processing programs offer spelling verification using system-supplied and user-enhanced dictionaries. (A small term authority list may be added to such a dictionary.) Spelling verification will locate most typographical errors and spelling mistakes, but it will not be able to verify accuracy of indexing or locate homonym errors.

Ongoing Proofreading

Even with careful quality control procedures at input, some typographical or factual errors will creep into your database. Information may go out of date, subject descriptors might change, or a value may be valid for one record but not for another. A program of ongoing proofreading and correcting is therefore necessary. An error report form available to users and to system maintenance personnel will encourage correction of both typographical and intellectual errors. Corrections can be scheduled as a part of the regular update process.

Printing portions of the inverted index will highlight typographical errors or problems with inconsistent input in controlled fields. Such printing may be scheduled on a regular basis. Inconsistencies that occur in many records are more likely to affect retrieval adversely than infrequent spelling errors. Setting priorities for error correction might therefore be desirable, so an undue amount of time is not devoted to correcting rarely occurring errors.

The success of all error detection and correction procedures is dependent on how easy it is to make corrections to the existing database. An important criterion for software evaluation is the ease of correction procedures if ongoing quality control is important to you.

Systematic, ongoing proofreading and error correction is time-consuming and can be expensive. It should not substitute for quality control at input. Speaking from the commercial database producer perspective, Ron Kaminecki stated in a February 1984 letter to the editor of *Database* magazine:

> . . . it is better to correct the error at the time of input before the number of items gets out of hand than it is to correct a very large database. . . . Such editing can be accomplished by verification (i.e., keystroke the data twice by two different operators) and by more careful human "eyeballing." It is true that these techniques are expensive, but it is much cheaper to catch such errors early on. . . .

FURTHER READING

Beck, S.J. "Alternatives to Online Downloading." In *Proceedings of the Online '85 Conference,* 31–36. Weston, Conn.: Online, Inc., 1985.

Buckland, Lawrence F. *Data Input for Publishers.* Littleton, Mass.: Inforonics, 1984.

Eddison, Betty. "Database Design: Computerizing Your Information." *Database* 9 (April 1986): 85–87.

Ellingen, Dana C. "Database Design: Quality Control and Your Database." *Database* 9 (June 1986): 102–105.

Garman, Nancy. "Downloading . . . Still a Live Issue?" *Online* 10 (July 1986): 15–31.

Gee, Ralph. "Quality Control in Online Databases." *Aslib Proceedings* 35 (June/July 1983): 239–248.

Kaminecki, Ron. "Cleaning up Dirty Data: An Awesome Task." *Database* (February 1984): 5.

Miller, David C. "Running With CD-ROM." *American Libraries* 17 (November 1986): 754–756.

Norton, Nancy. " 'Dirty Data': A Call for Quality Control." *Online* (January 1981): 40–41.

Ralph, R.D. "Downloading and Data Conversion: Doing it Yourself." In *Proceedings of the Online '85 Conference,* 247–253. Weston, Conn.: Online, Inc., 1985.

Tenopir, Carol. "CD-ROM in 1986." In *Library and Information Science Annual,* Volume 3. Littleton, Colo.: Libraries Unlimited, 1987: 21–25

Tenopir, Carol. "Database Subsets." *Library Journal* 110 (May 15, 1985): 42–43.

Tenopir, Carol. "Online Searching With a Microcomputer: Downloading Issues." *Microcomputers for Information Management* 2 (June 1985): 77–89.

Tenopir, Carol. "Quality Control." *Library Journal* 112 (February 15, 1987): 124–125.

10
Documentation

Although this is one of the last chapters, it does not mean that documentation should be put off until the rest of your database project is complete. Documenting your database is an ongoing process that started with the feasibility study. It is an integral part of the database design and creation process. Parts of your feasibility study, data dictionary, indexing rules, and data entry form are all early versions of documentation. They have been used and revised all along in the database design. This chapter discusses how to polish, supplement, and organize this documentation into a finished product.

Database documentation is of two types: printed manuals or online help. Both are discussed in this chapter. More details on writing manuals can be found in the books cited in the Further Readings section.

MANUALS

When you purchased your software, you should have received a manual covering installation of the program and some instructions on how to design databases using this program. If a programming language was a part of the package, the manual might include extensive programming instructions. As you set up your database, you probably appreciated good software documentation (or cursed poor documentation) of the package you were using. The documentation you write for your database will not replace the system documentation, but it will allow you to focus on your users and on your application to create a good customized product.

Because they already exist, system technical level or design level manuals are usually not rewritten by the database creator. They will not be discussed here. If you used a DBMS package, however, you may have done extensive programming in the DBMS language. Programming documentation is outside the main scope of this book, but is described briefly later in this chapter.

You will probably just need to write documentation that describes your particular application. It should not duplicate the existing documentation, but it may make references back to the system manual. Your manual may be separated into two sections (or into two separate manuals) corresponding to two separate audiences. There should be a section for database staff (inputters, indexers, and so on) and users of the database.

User Manual

The user manual is important both to tell users how to do specific functions and to illustrate how to solve a particular problem. That means it will sometimes be used as a beginning level tutorial and sometimes as a reference tool to answer a specific question. It should cover everything that users may need to know about the database and the software, but in as succinct a manner as possible. Remember that most people do not like to read manuals; many would prefer to sit down at the computer and figure things out for themselves. The manual can provide a back-up or trouble-shooting guide for these people. It should also serve those who would rather read instructions before trying things out.

Readability. The tone, style, and content of your user manual depends on who the primary users of your database are. As an inhouse database designer, you have an advantage over the software documentation authors because your users were identified in your feasibility study. A manual written for elementary school students must, obviously, differ from that written for engineers. If you have little experience with technical writing, you may want to test your writing style before completing your final draft.

Readability can be measured with simple tests developed for this purpose, such as Gunning's Fog Index or the Flesch Reading Ease Formula. The Gunning Fog Index compares the average number of words in a sentence with the percent of difficult words. The resulting score translates to educational level and tells how difficult a text is to understand. Gunning recommended readability be kept at or below the twelfth grade level except for highly technical material.

Figure 10.1 shows how to compute the Fog Index and the Flesch Reading Ease Formula and how to interpret their scores. The first passage in Figure 10.2, from an actual computer operating system users manual, has a Fog Index of 21 and a score of 15.9 using the Flesch Reading Ease Formula. Not even a college graduate could be expected to understand that passage. On the other hand, if you apply

FIGURE 10.1   Gunning's Fog Index and Flesch Reading Ease Formula

FOG INDEX

The Formula:
1. Choose a sample of 100 words or more.
2. Divide the number of words by the number of sentences to find the average number of words in a sentence.
3. Count the words of three or more syllables. Do not count proper nouns. Divide the total by the number of words in the sample. This gives you the percent of difficult words in the sample.
4. Add the average number of words in a sentence to the percent of difficult words.
5. Multiply the resulting total from step 4 by 0.4. This will give you the Fog Count or Index of the sample.

INTERPRETING THE INDEX

	FOG INDEX	*READING LEVEL*
	17	College graduate
	16	College senior
	15	College junior
	14	College sophomore
DANGER LINE	13	College freshman
	12	High school senior
	11	High school junior
	10	High school sophomore
	9	High school freshman
EASY READING RANGE	8	Eighth grade
	7	Seventh grade
	6	Sixth grade

FLESCH READING EASE FORMULA

The Formula:
1. Unless you are testing a whole piece of writing, take samples.
2. Count the words in each sample up to 100. Count contractions and hyphenated words as one word.
3. Count the syllables in the 100-word sample, or if you are testing a whole piece of writing, count the number of syllables per 100 words.
4. Find the average number of words per sentence. In a 100-word sample, find the sentence that ends nearest the 100-word mark. Count the number of sentences up to that point and divide the number of words by the number of sentences.

FIGURE 10.1, Cont'd.

---

5. Find the "reading ease" score by computing the following formula: [.39(average words/sentence) + 11.8(average syllables/word)] - 15.59.

INTERPRETING THE SCORE

READING EASE SCORE	DESCRIPTION OF STYLE
0 to 30	Very difficult
30 to 50	Difficult
50 to 60	Fairly difficult
60 to 70	Standard
70 to 80	Fairly easy
80 to 90	Easy
90 to 100	Very easy

---

the Fog Index to the introduction of the inhouse database manual in the second passage in Figure 10.2, you'll find it measures at the tenth grade level. Both the Reading Ease Formula and Gunning's Fog Index can be computed manually, or software can be purchased that will compute readability on word processing files.

FIGURE 10.2   Measuring Readability

1

The second IRPC shown in Figure 13 uses the controlling identifier "C" to generate a number of single byte constants with corresponding labels. It is important to observe that although the controlling variable was typed in lower case it has been translated to upper case during assembly. Further, note that the string '&C' occurs within the group and, since the controlling variable is enclosed in string quotes, it must occur next to an ampersand operator and be typed in upper case for the substitution to occur properly. On each iteration of the IRPC, a label is constructed through concatenation, and a "DB" is generated with the corresponding character from the character-list.

It should be pointed out that substitution of the controlling identifier by its associated value could cause infinite substitution if the controlling identifier is the same as the character from the character-list. For this reason, the macro assembler performs the substitution and then moves along to read the next segment of the program, rather than re-reading the substituted text for another possible occurrence of the controlling identifier.

WORDS: 178, SENTENCES: 6, DIFFICULT WORDS: 41, FOG INDEX: 21
AVERAGE WORDS PER SENTENCE: 29, AVERAGE SYLLABLES PER WORD
(FIRST 100 WORDS): 1.71, FLESCH READING EASE: 15.9

F<small>IGURE</small> 10.2, Cont'd.

2

INTRODUCTION

The JOBS database is a collection of job announcements for all types of library work. It contains short versions of the ads received by the School of Library and Information Studies from employers all over the world. Full versions of the ads are kept in the folder file next to the database. They are filed by document number found in the database version of the ad.

At any time the database contains approximately 250 ads. Once they are entered into the database they are referred to as "records." The database is updated on a weekly basis, at which time outdated ads or records are removed and new ones added. The exact number of records in the database will vary.

The JOBS database has been set up with a program called Sci-Mate. As you search for job ads, the Sci-Mate system will ask you how you want to proceed. Options will be displayed on the screen. This program makes it easy to search for types of jobs, types of libraries, or places simply by entering the words that describe them. Once you complete a search, any of the records found may be displayed or printed.

This manual leads you through the steps to follow to locate job ads of possible interest to you. If you are new to the Sci-Mate system, it is a good idea to start with Part I: Getting Started.

GETTING STARTED

Diskettes needed are:
1. DOS disk
2. Sci-Mate Manager Disk
3. JOBS Data Disk

Now:
1. Insert the DOS disk in Drive A
2. Turn on the computer (on the right side).
3. Turn on the monitor (on the top).

An "A>" will appear on the screen. This is called a prompt and it is your cue from the computer to take the next action:

4. Remove the DOS disk from drive A
5. Insert the Sci-Mate Manager disk in drive A and
6. Insert the JOBS data disk in Drive B

Next, type the word scimate and press the Enter key. Soon a Sci-Mate welcome screen will appear.

Go to the next section for instructions on searching.

Organization of the Manual. If your audience is of mixed levels, you must include basic explanatory information as well as advanced material. It should be presented in a way that is informative, yet not condescending. One way to accommodate a wide variety of user levels is to separate the text by levels. Explain at the beginning of the manual who needs to read which sections. You might organize the information into information essential to everyone, background information for beginners (including a tutorial), advanced information for experienced users.

The user manual should be organized in a way that is logical for the users, not necessarily for the database designer. One model for the contents of a user manual is given in Figure 10.3. The *table of contents* should be detailed enough that users can find specific functions or commands. This means you should divide your manual into small sections and assign meaningful headers or titles to each section.

The *introduction* defines the purpose and contents of the database, describes the software, and tells the reader what to expect in the manual. An introduction need not be lengthy, in fact a succinct statement is better. The example in Figure 10.2 conveys information about the software, the database, and the contents of the manual, but only takes one-half page.

The next section should be a simple *tutorial* that leads the novice through the search process. The tutorial provides step-by-step instructions for how to accomplish a simple task, such as conducting a single word search and printing the resulting citations. It includes sample searches and sample records from your database. Users may first read the tutorial and then try their own searches online or they might log on to the database and follow the examples in the tutorial. Feeling successful is important, so make sure that all of the examples in your tutorial work online as written in the manual.

The tutorial satisfies those users who would prefer to be led by the hand at first. It is also useful for people who learn better by example than by text. Your manual will be used mostly as a reference manual, however, to assist users who want to find out how to do a specific task or get out of a particular problem. The heart of the user manual thus is the sections that give details of commands and functions. Some users will read these sections before they begin to use the database, but most will refer only to those sections they need, when they need them.

Figure 10.3 separates these into basic features and advanced features. The basic section might include: logging on, search com-

FIGURE 10.3 Sample Contents of a User Manual

1. TABLE OF CONTENTS
2. INTRODUCTION
   2.1 Goals and objectives of database
   2.2 Content of database
   2.3 Organization of manual
3. HOW TO FIND SOMETHING
   3.1 Getting on the system
   3.2 Simple subject searching
   3.3 Displaying results
   3.4 Contents of the records
   3.5 Getting off the system
4. BASIC COMMANDS
   4.1 Subject searching
   4.2 Combining terms
       4.2.1 AND
       4.2.2 OR
       4.2.3 Using AND and OR together
   4.3 Truncation
   4.4 Searching for authors
   4.5 Searching by dates
       4.5.1 Range searching
       4.5.2 Searching with comparison operators
   4.6 Word proximity searching
       4.6.1 Word adjacency
       4.6.2 Words within a specified range
   4.7 Modifying your search
5. ADVANCED COMMANDS
   5.1 Refining search results
       5.1.1 If you retrieve no documents
       5.1.2 If you retrieve too many documents
   5.2 More on logical operators
       5.2.1 NOT
       5.2.2 Nesting operators with parentheses
   5.3 Viewing the inverted index
   5.4 Custom-generated reports
6. TROUBLE SHOOTING
   6.1 Why things go wrong
   6.2 Error messages
   6.3 When to check the system manual
7. GLOSSARY (Optional)
8. INDEX

mands, Boolean operations, proximity searching, simple display, and logging off. The advanced command section may cover more complex search features, sorting, and creation of customized displays or reports. Optionally, if the general software documentation is good, you might want to refer users to the advanced command section for any complicated features.

The *trouble shooting* section is used only as a reference manual. When something goes wrong, when an error message is displayed, or the system goes down, the user will turn to trouble shooting (or the database administrator) for help. This section should refer to the original software system manual for software failures rather than attempt to duplicate that manual.

Many good manuals include a glossary that defines database jargon and terms encountered in the manual. For an inhouse database, it can also define special terminology that might be encountered in the data. Including a glossary or not is an individual decision based on the level of your users and the availability of human assistance. An index is not an optional feature, however. Manuals without indexes are frustrating to use and sometimes virtually useless. Always include an index in a user manual.

Illustrations. Examples and illustrations help convey your information. You might not have professionally produced graphics, but plenty of examples of actions and their results with records taken from your application are the best illustrations. (The examples should always be specific to your database and not just copied from the system supplied manual.) Simple line drawings might supplement the examples. Since this manual is for inhouse consumption only, illustrations do not have to be of professional quality.

Maintainer's Manual

The other manual needed for an inhouse database is the manual that describes the indexing and data entry functions. The audience for this manual is the person or persons responsible for the continued upkeep of the database.

Figure 10.4 provides a suggested table of contents for the maintainer's manual. Some parts may be the same as parts of the user manual. The *introduction,* for example, may contain an identical explanation of the software and the database. Only the part explaining the purpose and contents of the manual will differ. The searching section may reproduce or refer back to the three sections on search features in the user manual.

FIGURE 10.4 Sample Contents of a Maintainer's Manual

1. TABLE OF CONTENTS
2. INTRODUCTION
    2.1 Goals and objectives of database
    2.2 Content of database
    2.3 Organization of the manual
    2.4 Why maintenance is important
3. HOW TO CREATE RECORDS
    3.1 Field structure
    3.2 Description of each field
        3.2.1 Definition of each
        3.2.2 Content of each
        3.2.3 Do rules for content apply?
    3.3 Value-Added Fields
        3.3.1 Subject descriptors
            3.3.1.1 Authority control
            3.3.1.2 How to index
            3.3.1.3 Rules for indexing
        3.3.2 Abstracts
            3.3.2.1 Purpose and style of abstracts
            3.3.2.2 Examples of abstracts
    3.4 How to fill out an input form
4. HOW TO ADD RECORDS
    4.1 How to follow the input form
    4.2 Interaction with indexing personnel
    4.3 Quality control
        4.3.1 Verifying input
        4.3.2 Proofreading
        4.3.3 What if the input form is wrong?
    4.4 Updating the inverted indexes
    4.5 Batch additions
5. SEARCHING
    5.1 How input affects searching
    5.2 How users will be searching
    5.3 How to search for known items
        5.3.1 Accession number searching
        5.3.2 Author searching
        5.3.3 Title searching
6. CORRECTIONS
    6.1 Locating the correct record
    6.2 How to make corrections
        6.2.1 Screen editing
        6.2.2 Inserting text
    6.3 Deleting records
    6.4 Updating the inverted indexes

Figure 10.4, Cont'd.

---

7. TROUBLE SHOOTING
   7.1 Why things go wrong
   7.2 Error messages
   7.3 When to turn to the system manual
8. INDEX

The sections that are unique to the maintainer's manual are the sections on creating records and inputting records. Together, they describe the processes of getting information into the database from both the intellectual decision-making viewpoint and the mechanical data entry viewpoint.

Much of "How to Create Records" is based on the editorial decisions described in Chapter 5 and the structural decisions outlined in Chapter 6. Your data dictionary forms the outline for this section because it includes descriptions of all fields, what their contents should be, rules for standardization of input, and references to any authority files or thesauri. The manual expands on this information. "How to Create Records" may include the actual authority lists if they are original (and not too long) or it may merely refer to them.

Step-by-step instructions on how to input records according to your record structure make up the section on "How to Input Records." It is not a manual on how to create a record structure or design a new database; presumably that information is included in the software documentation. Your manual instead refers to the unique fields and structure of this particular database and illustrates how the input features of the software package can be used for the specific application. There should be plenty of specific examples and illustrations.

Programming Documentation

If your system design required original programming, either in a standard programming language or in a DBMS programming language, you will need to write programming documentation also. A well-designed and well-written program using today's programming languages will be to a large extent self documenting. The liberal inclusion of informative comments in the source code, the use of descriptive variable names, and the logically structured modular approach to program development will all make for programs that are easier to read and understand, and to modify if necessary.

A source language program listing is an essential part of the documentation. In addition to the statements that actually do the data processing, the program should have a comment section at the beginning describing the program, what it does, the basic algorithm used, requirements for running it (data files, data format, operating system, and other associated programs or supporting materials, and so on). This comment header should also record the name of the programmer, the date the program was finished, any modifications made to the program, and dates these modifications were made. Major modules within the program should also be headed with descriptive comments.

In addition to the source code listing, program documentation normally includes a narrative description of the program, what it does, how it works, what is needed to make it work, any limitations, and sample data and output. Basically what is needed in programming documentation is information that will help a programmer (perhaps the same one who wrote the original code) to understand the program well enough to modify it. It is the rare program that is not modified after it is installed, either because of enhancements to the original design, changes in other components of the system, or the surfacing of some well hidden bugs. Good documentation will make software maintenance easier and therefore less costly.

Reproducing the Manuals

The content of your manuals is the most important consideration, but physical layout and appearance also have an impact on readability. You may have few options for reproducing an inhouse manual. The printer you use for word processing may determine the choice of typefaces, and the photocopy machine may be your only option for reproduction. These realities may limit the size of your manual to 8½-by-11-inch (or 4-by-5½-inch) paper and your colors to black and white. Illustrations may have to be kept to a minimum, although examples do not have to be limited. (For a range of less limited layout and reproduction options, see Jonathan Price's *How To Write a Computer Manual: A Handbook of Software Documentation.*)

Even with these constraints you have some control over the physical appearance of your manual. Things that will help readability include ample white space and wide margins, text set off with bullets or in lists, boxes or highlights drawn around important messages, use of boldface or capital letters to differentiate computer from human responses, and a binder or sturdy cover.

Price lists a number of elements that must be designed in any manual and over which you have control:

- Asides: is a special format required for information that is not essential?
- Figures: this includes illustrations, diagrams, and maps.
- Headings: usually two or three levels indicated by capital letters and upper and lower case letters.
- Icons: for instance, drawings that indicate disk drives, or computer elements referred to regularly.
- Key terms: should they be highlighted using boldface type, underlines, or italics?
- Lists: should they be bulleted or numbered?
- Marginal glosses: should key term definitions appear in the margins?
- Prefatory material: disclaimers, copyright, and trademark information will have to be handled specially.
- Running heads: use chapter titles and section titles.
- Sample screens: will you use photographs of actual screens or reset them.
- Special keys: should you use a special symbol for the RETURN key and for the ARROW keys?
- Subscripts and superscripts: if you have a lot of mathematical formulas, you'll have to set them off from the regular text.
- Summaries and quick reference material: should they set in smaller type?
- Tables of contents: you will have to show the difference between various levels of headings. Should there be chapter tables of contents?
- Tables.
- Text.
- Text that the readers must type. Should you use a special typeface so that each letter looks like the key the reader will type?
- Titles.
- Tutorial text: should this be set in two columns?
- Warnings: should these be printed in color or set in boldface or italics to alert the reader?

Other Printed Aids

The user manual is often supplemented with aids that make it easy for users to find the answers they need. These aids summarize system commands and functions in a succinct fashion, so users do not have to check the manual for simple functions. Some aids to consider include quick reference cards, folding quick reference charts, and function key labels.

Quick Reference Cards. Quick reference cards summarize the key commands and procedures needed to search the database. They list each important command and give an example of how to use it. They contain only enough information to get a user started searching and keep him searching. They supplement looking things up in the much larger user manual. The quick reference card is usually vest pocket size, so it is easily picked up and carried by users. For an inhouse database, it may be any convenient size up to 8½-by-11-inches.

Quick Reference Charts. The folding quick reference chart serves the same purpose as the card, but it is meant to be kept at the database workstation. Commands are summarized on a stiff cardboard chart, which is then folded so it will stand up on the desk top or computer top. Users can quickly glance at the chart to find proper command sequence and format.

Function Key Labels. Most database software written for the IBM-PC or compatibles makes use of function keys for common operations. If your microcomputer is being used primarily for your inhouse database, it may be helpful to make a function key template that labels and defines each key's function. This template fits around the function keys.

ONLINE DOCUMENTATION

Although it is seldom sufficient by itself, online documentation is an important part of the total documentation of a database. Online documentation includes online help messages, error messages, and online tutorials. Unfortunately, many of the software packages used for textual databases do not allow the database designer to add any online messages. You evaluated a package's help and error messages as part of the software evaluation, so you know how good the general system help is. The system may have a general online tutorial that teaches how to search a sample database. Although this tutorial will not teach users about your particular database structure and contents, it may be useful to teach general searching commands.

If your software package does allow you to add online documentation, you will be able to create customized online tutorials and other help for your particular database and users. When designing any type of online documentation, many of the general rules of good documentation and style apply. For a detailed discussion of online documentation see Brockmann in the Further Readings section. Some hints specific to the online form are given below.

- Keep each screen short and simple. Too many words on any one screen are hard on the eyes and quickly get boring.
- Keep screens uncluttered. Break up the text with ample blank space and do not try to put too many different kinds of information on any one screen.
- Use highlighting, boxes, and windowing with discretion. They are useful tools to set off important text, but overuse is distracting and confusing.
- Use color consistently and with discretion. Color is a useful tool to differentiate between types of information. Error messages, for example, might always be in blue, help screens bordered in red. Too much color or inconsistent color is confusing and hard on the eyes.
- Keep screen formats consistent. If an action is required from the user, for example, always put the request for action in the same place on the screen. If error messages are highlighted with a single-line box, never use a double-line box for an error message.
- Use multi-level help screens. The first level should be short, containing only the essential information. The second level can go into more detail for those who need it.
- Make sure that users can get into help mode at any time, and that it is clear how to get out of help mode.

FURTHER READINGS

Brockmann, John. *Writing Better Computer User Documentation*. New York: John Wiley and Sons, 1986.

Flesch, Rudolf F. "A New Readability Yardstick," *Journal of Applied Psychology* 32 (June 1968): 221–233.

Gunning, Robert. *The Technique of Clear Writing*. New York: McGraw-Hill, 1952.

Howard, Jim. "What Is Good Documentation?" *Byte* 6 (March 1981): 132–140.

McKee, John B. "Computer User Manuals in Print: Do They Have a Future?" **Asterisk* 12 (August 1986): 11–19.

Price, Jonathan. *How To Write a Computer Manual: A Handbook of Software*

Documentation. Menlo Park, Calif.: Benjamin/Cummings Publishing Company, 1984.

Spear, Barbara. *How to Document Your Software.* Blue Ridge Summit, Penn.: Tab Books, 1984.

Weiss, Edmond H. *How to Write a Usable User Manual.* Philadelphia: ISI Press, 1985.

See various issues of: **Asterisk,* the newsletter of the ACM Special Interest Group for Systems Documentation.

11
The Future

In looking at the near future for textual databases it is fairly safe to project current trends. The capabilities of larger systems will continue to migrate to microcomputer applications. It is harder to predict the impact of market forces that will determine in the end what mix will emerge from the various technological possibilities.

All of the technologies used in database systems are experiencing rapid development. Much of what we take for granted in today's systems would have been impossible or prohibitively expensive just a few years ago. At the same time technology is developing, the user interface and human factors are beginning to receive serious attention from researchers. Further work in this area will be needed to provide guidance for how best to use the potential that we are creating with the technology.

The technologies of database software can be grouped into four major areas: computers and electronics, data storage, communications, and software. Each of these areas offers promise of significant improvements over current database systems. In combination, advances in all of these areas can make very dramatic improvements possible.

COMPUTERS AND ELECTRONICS

Microcomputers continue to grow in power and decrease in cost. The result is that use of microcomputers is becoming almost commonplace. This progress is due primarily to advances in microelectronics technology.

Microelectronics

Integrated circuits were first introduced around 1960. Since that time the number of components that can be put on a single chip has doubled each year. As an example, in the mid 1970s memory chips had a capacity of 1 K bits. Ten years later 256 K bit chips were common. Similar increases in densities of other chips (CPU, I/O circuitry, and others) have resulted in continuing decreases in the size, cost, and number of individual parts of microcomputers, and an increase in power and reliability. This trend can be expected to continue. The latest versions of microprocessors offer significantly increased processing speed over the previous generation and compare favorably with large minicomputers of just a few years ago. They offer enough power to support multitasking and multiuser systems, while maintaining compatibility with existing software.

A move from chip technology to wafer technology in microelectronic manufacturing promises still more reliable and compact computers. Instead of making chips of about one-quarter-inch-square with hundreds of thousands of transistors and using several chips in a computer, millions of transistors are put on a wafer a few inches in diameter. The circuits are designed to be self repairing. If defects are introduced in manufacturing or develop later, the computer will continue to work.

The replacement of silicon by other materials such as gallium arsenide offers higher speeds and lower power consumption. One result of this will be still more powerful battery operated portable computers.

Database Machines

The low cost of microprocessors is making possible the development of special purpose database machines that employ multiple processors operating in parallel. Database machines offer the possibility of scanning large text files in a sequential fashion in reasonable times without the need for inverted indexes. This means that computer storage is kept to a minimum and changes to the database are immediately searchable. Database machines have been commercially available for several years, but at costs well above the microcomputer range. GESCAN 2, for example, is able to search text files at the rate of 2 million characters per second with Boolean logic, right and left truncation, word proximity, and partial matching capabilities.

STORAGE TECHNOLOGIES

Developments in storage technologies have been as exciting as those in electronics. Capacities continue to increase and costs continue to decrease. The older magnetic media have been joined by a variety of optical media.

Magnetic Storage

Magnetic disk storage has been the mainstay of database storage. Recording densities have increased dramatically, going from about 100 K bytes per 5¼-inch floppy disk in the late 1970s to several megabytes per disk by the late 1980s. Densities for hard disks have also increased, while prices have dropped. Further increases in magnetic recording densities can be expected, keeping this technology competitive with the newer optical media for a few years at least. The high capacity and low cost expected in the near future mean that record size and indexing overhead will be less critical factors in database design.

Optical Storage

Optical storage media offer much higher capacities than do the magnetic media, although the access speed is slower. A variety of formats and recording methods are being used and developed. Read-only media are a more mature part of this technology. This does not compete with magnetic storage since it cannot be erased or written to. As mentioned in Chapter 9, CD ROM and other read-only formats make possible the affordable publication and distribution of massive amounts of data and allow local searching of publicly available databases. This kind of database publishing will undoubtedly grow. As it does, it will impact data entry and conversion options.

Write once (WORM) optical technology and especially erasable read/write optical recording will compete with magnetic storage for inhouse database applications. For many textual database applications the lack of erasing capabilities may be considered an asset. Erasable optical media are now available commercially at competitive costs on a per megabyte basis. Magneto-optical recording appears to be the most viable approach to erasable optical storage. While this technology records by altering the magnetic orientation of the recording medium as does magnetic recording, lasers are used in both writing and reading.

Other optical media and formats are likely to emerge. Some variations that have already been introduced include laser cards and slides. Smaller formats such as cards are attractive to software developers since they offer a low cost method of distribution in a form not easily copied. Standards are needed and are being developed for optical media. Such standards will help assure a wider market for published data on optical media.

COMMUNICATIONS TECHNOLOGIES

Data transmission through communication networks, both local area networks (LANs) and wide area networks (mainly the packet switching value-added networks or VANs) is vital to current database activity. Searching and downloading from remote databases makes use of the VANs; sharing local databases within an organization can be accomplished with a LAN as discussed in Chapter 2.

Local Area Networks

Local area networks have evolved since the mid-1970s and are only now becoming cost effective, easy to install, and easy to use systems for microcomputer based networks. Data transmission rates in LANs range up to about ten megabytes per second. Much of the database software currently available does not work on networks, although the software producers are quickly upgrading their products and offering versions that will run on LANs. Since this is a relatively new technology, there is considerable room for improvements. Costs are likely to drop rapidly, while performance and ease of installation and use will improve. Having your database on a LAN means more administrative work for such tasks as assigning passwords and controlling access.

Value-Added Networks

Value-added networks and the telephone system on which they depend offer much lower data rates than do LANs. Currently 1,200 bits per second (BPS) modems are common, with some higher speed modems in the range of 2,400 to 9,600 BPS being used with the existing analog telephone lines. New digital telephone lines offer data transmission rates of 56,000 BPS (56 KBPS). Data rates of one billion bits per second have been achieved with optical fibers in the laboratory. Optical fibers have a theoretical upper limit a million times higher still. It has been estimated that all of man's recorded knowledge amounts to about 10 to the 15th power bits. At the theoretical limit of fiber optics, all recorded knowledge could be transmitted in one second.

The discrepancy between data storage and current telephone line data transmission capacity is pointed out by the fact that the sending of the contents of a CD ROM disk over a 1,200 BPS modem would require about 53 days. At 56 KBPS the transmission would take about 27 hours, comparable to the time required to send the disk by air express courier service. On the other hand, current communication satellites and fiber optics systems can send data much faster than current disk storage devices can write.

The continued development of a worldwide telecommunications network, including terrestrial and submarine fiber optic cables and new generations of communications satellites, will make data communication costs virtually unaffected by distance. This should make possible the development of distributed database systems with components scattered over a wide geographic range. Electronic document delivery, either as ASCII text or by telefacsimile, will become more cost effective.

SOFTWARE

When compared with hardware, advances in software have been much more modest. Still we are seeing steady progress in the development of retrieval systems and the programming languages, algorithms, and operating systems on which they are built.

Programming Languages and Tools

There has been slow but certain progress in programming language development. Structured programming is now the accepted standard, and modern programming languages are designed to facilitate this approach. The result is programs that are easier to debug and to update and maintain. Along with improved languages, we have improving programming environments—better editors, compilers, and debuggers, for example. In addition to the traditional procedure oriented languages, we are seeing what are being referred to as "fourth generation languages" or "problem oriented languages," which are easier to program for the particular kinds of applications for which they are designed.

Artificial Intelligence

Expectations for artificial intelligence (AI) have been greater than its achievements thus far. Many current software packages, however, make use of AI technology to some extent. The area of AI most well developed in terms of practical applications is that of expert systems. Rather than storing all pertinent relationships in a database as individual data items, expert systems store the basic relationships and infer others based on rules that are stored in a *knowledge base*. Some information retrieval systems based on expert systems have been developed. So far these have for the most part been experimental, but practical applications of this approach can be expected to proliferate.

Research and development toward "fifth generation" computers, which incorporate AI concepts, aim to result in computers that can deal with natural language and support voice input. This will certainly have an impact on textual database systems when it is achieved.

Other Approaches

Meanwhile a number of other approaches, mostly in the experimental stage now, are likely to find practical application. Several non-Boolean approaches to information retrieval, some of which were briefly mentioned at the end of Chapter 3, offer promise of better retrieval performance while being easier for the average user to interact with.

HUMAN FACTORS

With all the attention that AI is getting, it is easy to overlook the natural intelligence factor in database systems. It is clear from research that has been done in human-machine interface that the design of the interface can make a large difference in the effectiveness of the interaction. Productivity can vary by a factor of two or more depending on the interface. Research in human-machine interface is an area that has only recently received much attention. Continued research into human factors will be needed to produce truly effective and easy to use systems.

CONCLUSIONS

In summary, we can expect continued dramatic increases in computing power, storage capacity, and data transmission rates, with decreasing costs. We can expect steady progress in software capabilities. The combination of hardware and software advances will result in dramatic increases in performance and ease of use on inhouse database systems.

In 1981, Gerald Lundeen wrote:

> One can envision the day when a researcher will turn to his own information system to access his personal files, his invisible college network, departmental files, his local library or information center, centralized bibliographic utilities, and electronically published journal systems.

For many researchers that day has arrived. All of the functions mentioned above can now be done with a personal computer. What was envisioned, however, was an information system that smoothly integrated all of the functions, making the transition and the movement of data from one level to another easy and natural. We still must make more progress before we achieve this level of integration. We might add to the above picture such things as natural language interaction with voice input and speech synthesis as well as high resolution graphics and audiovisual output. In light of current progress this is not an unreasonable expectation.

FURTHER READINGS

Fox, Edward A. "Information Retrieval: Research into New Capabilities." In Lambert, Steve and Ropiequet, Suzanne, eds. *CD/ROM: The New Papyrus,* 143–174. Redmond, Wash.: Microsoft Press, 1986.

Lambert, Steve and Ropiequet, Suzanne. *CD/ROM: The New Papyrus.* Redmond, WA: Microsoft Press, 1986.

Lancaster, F.W. *Libraries and Librarians in an Age of Electronics.* Arlington, Va.: Information Resources Press, 1982.

Lancaster, F.W. and Neway, Julie M. "The Future of Indexing and Abstracting Services." *Journal of the American Society for Information Science* 33 (May 1982): 183–189.

Lundeen, Gerald. "Microcomputers in Personal Information Systems." *Special Libraries* 72(2) (April 1981): 127–137.

Salton, Gerard. "Some Characteristics of Future Information Systems." *SIGIR Forum* 18 (Fall 1985): 28–39.

Wise, Kensal, et al. *Microcomputers: A Technology Forecast and Assessment to the Year 2000.* New York: Wiley, 1980.

Appendix A
Database Design Case Study

SAMPLE PRELIMINARY FEASIBILITY STUDY

The Present Situation

Because of the rapid rate at which research is being done in the field of pediatric hematology/oncology, bound reference works are of extremely limited value. Pediatric hematologists/oncologists at the Pacific Medical Center [fictitious name] maintain a collection of files pertinent to their field. It includes articles torn out of journals, photocopies of articles, and reprints. The collection started in 1980.

The average document is 3–4 pages in length (3,000–4,000 words or 18,000 to 35,000 characters) and all are in English. Titles range from 30 characters to over 300. Approximately 90 percent of the titles fall within the range of 75–150 characters. Personal authors range from none to eleven. Most documents have three or fewer authors. Over 90 percent of the articles have author-written or editor-written abstracts at the beginning. These abstracts range in length from 250 words to over 1,000 words (1,500 characters to 8,000 characters.) Most fall within the range of 300–600 words.

The documents relate to all areas of pediatric hematology/oncology, including disease research, diagnosis, treatment plans, protocols, drug toxicity, and long-term morbidity. At present there are approximately 500 documents in this collection.

Research in the field of pediatric hematology/oncology is progressing at such a rapid rate that collections such as this are the only means to insure current literature is available for reference purposes. In addition, articles on these subject areas are found in a variety of journals: pediatric journals, cancer journals, hematology journals, pharmacology journals. Because the number of relevant articles in each of these journals is small, it is a savings of time and space to tear out only those articles that are relevant to pediatric hematology/oncology and dispose of the rest of the journal.

The collection is housed currently in one of the physician's offices at the hospital. It is kept in a file cabinet, which is about one-fourth full. There is room for the collection to triple.

The file was started and is maintained by one of the physicians. Approximately six articles are added per week. Current access is by disease name in alphabetical order. A few of the broader diseases (such as leukemia) have been broken down into subfiles identifying various aspects of the disease. The file is used by two pediatric hematologists/oncologists and the house staff—approximately eight people.

Almost all of the articles in this collection are indexed in the MEDLINE database. None of the users search MEDLINE, although they are all familiar with the database through the library and have used MeSH (Medical Subject Headings).

Establishing this collection has had several advantages. It is a ready-reference tool. The physician can obtain a treatment plan or other helpful information immediately when it is needed without leaving his office. It is helpful in the process of teaching the house staff because pertinent information can be immediately delivered to them.

Despite the improvements in information retrieval that the development of this collection has brought about, there are still some serious problems. Documents are easily lost in the file because of misfiling. The documents themselves contain no heading or number indicating where they are to be filed. While one user might file an article under a general heading, such as "leukemia," another might choose to file it under a subfile reflecting a particular aspect of the disease.

The greatest problem in dealing with this collection is the limited number of access points used to identify a document. In most cases, once the user has identified the file on the disease he or she is researching, he or she must manually go through that particular file to see if any articles are relevant to the aspect of the disease the user is seeking. For example, if a user desires information on the side-effects of a particular drug therapy for neuroblastoma, it might be necessary to scan all articles dealing with neuroblastoma to see which ones discuss therapy, and then further search this subset to see if the articles discuss side-effects of the therapy. The small size of the collection when it was first developed did not make this a significant problem. However, as the collection continues to grow, lack of access points is becoming a great handicap.

A new system is needed to manage this growing collection. Limited access to the documents is becoming a growing hindrance to retrieval of needed information. Because this collection is used to obtain very specific pieces of information, the user must have tools that allow the searching of very specific aspects of these diseases. A new system is also needed that will rely less on personal interpretation in locating documents, and therefore be more useful to the variety of individuals using the collection.

There currently is no hardware available in the pediatric department. However, paperwork has been completed for the purchase of an IBM-XT with a 20MB hard disk that is expected to be available within the year. It will be housed in the pediatric hematology/ oncology reception area. There are no inhouse programmers. However, it is felt that once the hardware arrives, the physicians will be free to purchase any software needed.

Desired System

A variety of methods of accessing these documents is important to the physicians. (See Figure A-1 on page 180 and Figure A-2 on pages 182–83.) Author and title access points will be necessary. In addition, the physicians want to be able to search for documents by disease and by names of drugs. They would like to be able to identify documents that deal with toxicity of particular drugs, long-term morbidity for various drugs and treatments, and those containing treatment plans and protocols for various diseases.

The desired system would contain the citation, ideally an abstract which would be searchable, and subjects describing the above information. The system would allow searching the entire record using the Boolean "and", "or" or "not" operators. There would need to be the ability to search by date for the purpose of weeding the collection.

Output would usually be online to the CRT screen or to a printer. Users would like to be able to select whether or not to display the abstract and would like to be able to sort results of a search alphabetically by author. In addition, it would be helpful to be able to print periodically a bibliography of articles on a disease or aspect of a disease so the physician could keep this hard copy list in his or her office for quick reference or incorporate it into a paper.

The most important feature as seen by the physicians is that they be able to identify quickly an article that deals with toxicity of a drug, long term morbidity of a treatment regime, or presents a protocol or treatment plan. It is imperative that they be able to search by connecting these above elements with a particular drug or disease.

Figure A.1   Record Definition and Field Specifications—
Preliminary Data Dictionary

Field Tag	Field Name	Type	Elements Repeat?	Value Req'd.	Controlled? How?	Searchable? Word or Phrase?	Sortable	Maximum Length	Fixed or Variable	Range	Average Length
LN	Location	a/n	no	yes	list	phrase	yes	7	fixed		
TI	Title	a/n	no	yes	no	word	yes	320	variable	30–320	125
AU	Author	a/n	yes	no	rules	phrase	yes	220	variable	0–220	35
JN	Journal	a/n	no	no	authority	phrase	no	40	variable	0–40	20
CI	Citation	a/n	no	no	no	no	no	45	variable	0–45	35
YR	Year	n	no	yes	rules	word	yes	4	fixed		
SU	Subject	a/n	yes	no	Thesaurus	word and phrase	no	140	variable	0–140	80
AB	Abstract	a/n	no	no	no	word	no	8,000	variable	0–8,000	500

Users of this database will be the two pediatric hematologists/ oncologists and the house staff. None have ever done database searching. However, all are familiar with MEDLINE, and most have had the medical librarian conduct searches for them. These eight users together would conduct an average of 1–3 searches per day on the inhouse database and would never require more than one person to be searching at one time. No intermediary would be present.

The system will be accessed in the reception area of the pediatric hematology/oncology offices. Although the collection has been maintained by the physician who first started the collection, a new secretary/database manager has been hired and it is hoped that she could soon take over this task. Physicians would submit to her the reprint to be included in the collection. On that reprint they could note important key terms, which they would want to use to retrieve the document. The database manager could assign those key terms and other terms relevant to the article as found in the MeSH. If the article had an abstract, it could be entered. Alternatively, the option of downloading records from MEDLINE will be explored.

The current number of documents in this collection is approximately 500. The collection is now growing at the rate of 5–6 documents per week (312 per year). It is anticipated that the collection would never exceed more than 2,000–2,500 documents because after four or five years the information would either no longer be relevant or would be available in current textbooks. Additions would need to be made weekly, and weeding would need to be done at least annually.

It is anticipated that this system will increase in size, but remain the same in form over the next one to five years. However, there may come a time when some changes would occur. These physicians belong to a study group called Pediatric Oncology Group (POG), headquartered on the East Coast. With many of the diseases, patients are registered with this group, and POG assigns experimental protocols to the patient. Much information is also shared among the POG members. There has been some experimenting with performing these tasks online with microcomputers and modems. It might be practical to integrate some of the protocols and information bulletins into this database.

VALUE-ADDED FIELDS AND AUTHORITY LISTS

Based on the needs analysis, two value-added fields were

Figure A.2 Field Structure of a Typical Journal Article

Field Tag	Field Name	Description of Content	Format or Source	Example
LN	Location	Unique identifying number that serves as a database control number and a file location number for each article	Use a control list to insure a unique number is assigned. The first two digits are the year of publication, the next four are a sequential accession number for each year. Place a hyphen after the year.	87-0234
TI	Title	The title of each article as given on the first page.	Enter the title as given on the first page of the article. If the downloaded title varies, make sure it is the same article and, if so, change the title to match the article in hand.	Chromosome Abnormalities in Down's Syndrome Patients with Acute Leukemia.
AU	Author	All of the personal authors of an article.	Enter each author's name with last name, comma, first name, middle name or middle initial as given on the first page. Separate multiple authors with a semicolon (or as specified by the software). Enter as many personal authors as are listed, in the order they are listed.	Breuer, Anthony; Steinherz, Peter G.

Code	Field	Description	Example
JN	Journal	The name of the journal in which the article is published.	Consult the journal authority list created for this project. This list has proper format for each journal and cross references from unused forms. New journals should be added in a form consistent with the list (as found in Medline if possible).	The New England Journal of Medicine JAMA Cancer
CI	Citation	Bibliographic information needed to identify or cite the article	Use the following format: volume (v.) number, issue (n.) number, page (pp.) numbers, and month.	v. 123, n. 3, pp. 123–145, September.
YR	Year	The year of publication	Use four digits	1987
SU	Subject	Subject words or phrases describing all major aspects of an article. Usually 5–7 headings suffice, but more are assigned if needed.	Select terms from the NLM MeSH supplemented by the database modifications and additional terms list. Inverted MeSH heading should be put into natural order. Separate each heading with a semicolon.	treatment; toxicity; cytosine arabinoside; myelocytic leukemia; acute lymphocytic leukemia
AB	Abstract	A summary description of the article, usually written by the author or by the journal editor.	Use abstracts at the beginning of each article or as found in Medline. If no abstracts exist, the physicians may choose to write one for high priority articles. Otherwise, leave this field blank.	

considered for inclusion in this database: abstracts and controlled vocabulary subject terms.

Abstracts were considered because:

- the physicians indicated that they would like abstracts to help them determine whether or not to retrieve an article,
- in the future, when the database is larger and is used by more people, the abstracts would be more important for relevance judging or to serve as a temporary substitute for an article if someone else had taken the article from the file or the file was not readily accessible to an individual,
- a searchable abstract offers more retrieval points.

Abstracts have several disadvantages for this database, however. In this technical subject they are typically between 300 to 600 characters and frequently much longer, thus using large amounts of disk storage space, and the physicians do not have time to write abstracts but the subject expertise required to write an abstract would make it difficult for the database administrator to write them.

Since the needs analysis found that approximately 90 percent of the articles include an author or editor-written abstract, a compromise is recommended. If an abstract is available, it should be entered into the database. If there is no abstract, physicians could write one for the highest priority articles. The remaining articles will be input without abstracts.

Controlled vocabulary subject terms were considered because:

- Controlled vocabulary terms allow for more precision in searching. Although that precision may not often be needed, when it is needed it is very important. For example, acute lymphocytic leukemia and acute lymphoblastic leukemia are the same disease. Some authors use one term and some the other. By always including acute lymphocytic leukemia in the subject field, articles on that topic can be retrieved no matter which term the author happened to use.
- Not all terms needed are found in the abstracts. In particular, the physicians noted important flags with which they wanted to be able to retrieve documents (such as toxicity, morbidity, and others). These terms would need to be added.
- If articles are indexed, the physicians can note terms they would like to see added to the records as their specific needs change.
- The indexing process will not take very long because the subject area of this collection is small and the number of documents added

per week is small. As the indexer becomes familiar with the topic, the assigning of terms will become easier.
- The physicians are familiar with the terminology used in the National Library of Medicine's Medical Subject Headings (MeSH.)

Controlled vocabulary subject terms have several disadvantages:

- Physicians were asked to look at indexing for a sample of the documents and add terms they wanted for retrieval purposes. Only 64 percent of the final terms came from MeSH. The rest were added to reflect the specialized needs of these users.
- The physicians did not like inverted subject terms (e.g., leukemia, myelocytic). They preferred to have them appear in natural order (e.g., myelocytic leukemia).
- Indexing initially will take time. In a small indexing study of these articles, it took an average of 15.2 minutes per article. Since there are approximately 500 articles currently in the collection, it would require about 126.7 hours to index the collection if this holds true. At the rate of growth of 5 articles per week, only 76 minutes of indexing per week would be needed to keep the file current.
- The database administrator is not a subject expert nor an experienced indexer. She may have difficulty with the task.

The advantages of controlled vocabulary indexing for this database outweigh the disadvantages. A compromise methodology for assigning the terms will eliminate many of the disadvantages.

Checking a sample of the collection online revealed that a majority (almost 85 percent) of these articles are found in the Medline database. Although the database administrator had never searched online before, it was a simple matter to teach her how to conduct a known item search in the database. Most of the titles are sufficiently specific and long so she just needed to search for a particular combination of words in the title to retrieve the one desired article. The time required to download the articles was minimal compared to indexing and inputting from scratch. Downloading is recommended as a cost effective way to build the database and do much of the indexing.

The database administrator can then edit the downloaded records and change headings to the form preferred by the users. When the physicians first submit an article to the database administrator for inclusion in the system, they can note the specific terms of importance to them that may not be found in the Medline record. If an abstract is on the article but not in the Medline record, it can be input by the database administrator.

The 15 percent of the articles not found in Medline will be indexed by the database administrator with help from the physicians. The medical librarian has offered to verify the records at first. It is expected that as the database administrator gains familiarity with the terminology and indexing process, she will be able to do it faster and less verification will be needed.

Indexing will be done at the level of the document to conform to NLM practices. Terms will be assigned for all major topics or topics of particular interest to the users. Most documents will need only five to seven subject terms but more can be added if necessary. An authority list of all changes to MeSH headings or terms added will be kept.

It was decided not to attempt authority control of authors' names because Medline enters authors as they appear on an article, and too much time would be spent trying to verify each one. There are frequently many authors per record.

An authority list will be maintained for journal names, however. Articles in this database come from relatively few journals, and users will probably frequently search on journal name. Cross references from unused to used names will be added to this list (e.g., Journal of the American Medical Association USE JAMA). Journal names in downloaded records will be verified by the database administrator using the journal name authority list.

SOFTWARE EVALUATION

Essential requirements for this application include: variable length fields (due to the wide range of values in several fields), the capability of having field lengths of up to 8,000 characters if needed, batch updating from a downloaded ASCII file, multiple values for fields, Boolean combination of terms, many searchable fields, and an easy-to-use query language. Several packages that might meet the needs of this database and these users were identified. Among the most likely candidates are: Reference Manager, Pro-Cite (with Biblio-links and Pro-Search), InMagic, and Sci-Mate.

Software evaluation forms for InMagic and Sci-Mate follow on pages 189–196. This is not to suggest that either of the other two packages would not be as acceptable. It should be noted that software evaluation varies with the application, and the choice for this project in no way suggests that the package not selected is a less satisfactory package for other applications. Also, software selection is in many ways subjective and the choice here should not be regarded as absolute.

Analysis of the Sci-Mate and InMagic Comparison

The Sci-Mate and InMagic programs were evaluated for use for the hematology/oncology database. Evaluation included reading reviews written about the software, reading of software documentation, and experimentation with the software itself (used by others in the community). Both programs met the minimum requirements. Most optional requirements could also be met, although at times that required some modifications to requirements or the use of the program. (For example, my record length might exceed the limitations of Sci-Mate, but Sci-Mate easily allows records to be linked.)

INMAGIC's advantages. In general, this appears to be a much more sophisticated program. It allows for more fields and longer records and fields. There is a great deal of flexibility in the way the records are constructed. Its searching powers are more flexible. It allows for range searching. It allows nesting for complex Boolean queries. Inverted indexes may be browsed. Report generation is extremely flexible.

INMAGIC's disadvantages. Because the system is more flexible, it does require more work in formulating both input and output requirements. Although the documentation is good and the online tutorial is excellent, it does assume at least some knowledge of computers and searching terminology in order to understand these directions. It is easy to batch transport downloaded records into InMagic, but the package does not include its own downloading module. A separate package would need to be purchased.

SCI-MATE's advantages. Sci-Mate allows for two methods of entering documents: keyboard input or downloading retrieved records using the Searcher portion of the program. The searcher allows users to search Medline through NLM, DIALOG, or BRS using a user friendly interface or the language of the host system. Documentation for Sci-Mate is written in clear and simple terms with many illustrations. No previous experience with searching or databases is needed. Searching features include left and right truncation, which would be helpful with chemical names used in drug therapy.

SCI-MATE's disadvantages. Sci-Mate's limited powers present some disadvantages. Searching powers exclude range searching, nesting (except for inverted files), and set building. Normally there are no online indexes to browse. When searching is completed, output flexibility is limited.

Choice of Software: Sci-Mate

It was obvious from my evaluation that InMagic is a more powerful and sophisticated program. However, Sci-Mate has some strong advantages that indicated to me it was a better choice for the needs of the hematology/oncology database and its users. First, the development of templates and inputting of data is less complicated, and the clear instructions of the documentation makes it feasible for someone with no computer background to carry out these tasks with a minimum of instruction.

Second, the use of the online Searcher may be a simple solution to data entry. The article can be located on Medline via the Searcher and be downloaded into the database. All that would need to be added in most cases would be the special terms or term variations the physicians want for their own use. A fringe benefit of this program would be that the Searcher could be used to meet some of the other information needs of the physicians.

The Editor allows enough flexibility to provide output lists in a useful format. Creation of formatted bibliographies in standard journal formats will be needed occasionally.

Finally, it was necessary to view the purpose of the database in relationship to the advantages and disadvantages of each program. The physicians' reason for wanting the database is to improve access to this small collection of articles. Their needs for report generation other than bibliographies are minimal. In most cases they only want to use the system to locate a document in the files. Because the collection is small and limited in subject matter, searches will tend to be simple and limited to a few terms. In view of these needs and the fact that inputting and maintenance will be performed by a secretary who is unfamiliar with bibliographic databases, the best choice would be one that could meet user needs in the simplest manner. Sci-Mate more than meets the needs of the users and appears to be the easier to use. It is therefore my choice of software for this particular project.

SOFTWARE EVALUATION FORM

Name of package: INMAGIC_____ Version: 7.0___
Producer: InMagic Inc._____
Contact Person:_____ Phone Number: 617-661-8124
Address: 238 Broadway, Cambridge, MA 02139_____

****

GENERAL CONSIDERATIONS:

    Number of records supported: no limit_____
    Number of fields per record: 75_____
    Restrictions on field lengths: none_____
    Variable length fields: yes_____
    Multiple Values per field: yes_____
    File Structures: sequential or inverted, user specifies
    Overhead: high: typically 300% but varies with indexing
    User designated Index fields: yes, up to 50_____
    DBMS or file manager: file manager_____
    Multiple user system: available at a much higher cost
    Comments: In-Magic appears very flexible in terms of
    fields and record structures. Overhead for indexes is high.

SCORE: ++
            0   1   2   3   4   5
    (UNACCEPTABLE) (POOR)   (FAIR) (AVERAGE) (GOOD) (EXCELLENT)

HARDWARE REQUIREMENTS:

    Turnkey system: no_____
    Brand/model required: IBM or compatible, also mini version
    Operating system(s): MS-DOS_____
    Memory required: 256K_____
    Peripherals required: none_____
    Other peripherals supported: hard disk recommended_____
    Dedicated hardware required: no_____
    Comments:_____

SCORE: ++
            0   1   2   3   4   5

DATA INPUT:

    Variety of input means: batch or keyboard
    Ease of input procedures: good
    New input identified: no
    User defined templates: yes
         Single or multiple templates per file: single
    Editing features: good
         Screen editor or line editor: screen
         Global changes: no, must dump to word processor
         Ease of edit commands: good
    Updating (batch or dynamic): at keyboard only dynamic
    Data verification: none
    Look-up tables: none
    Comments: Version 7.0 is a vast improvement in input
    over older versions.

SCORE: +++
         0   1   2   3   4   5

SEARCHING:

    Query language included: yes
    Menu driven or command: command
    Ease of learning: moderate, tutorial or help required
    Error messages: usually good, help available
    Set building: yes
    Boolean operators: AND, OR, NOT with nesting
    Proximity searching: no
    Comparison or arithmetic operators: comparison only
    Truncation: Right hand only
    Free text searching: yes
    All fields searchable: must specify field or fields to search
    Individual fields searchable: yes, must always specify
    Save and rerun searches: yes
    Vocabulary control: no
    Comments: Slightly cumbersome, must specify fields and
    query formats awkward. Not good for infrequent users.

SCORE: +++
         0   1   2   3   4   5

OUTPUT:

```
    Online screen display: default_____
    Report generator: powerful_____
         User defined formats: yes, unlimited_____
         System supplied formats: BiblioGuide includes many
         Ease of use: moderate_____
    Sorting: powerful_____
         User defined: yes and subsorts_____
         System supplied: 7 different sorting schemes_____
         Entire database or subset: both_____
    Arithmetic functions: In report generator can do basic
    Comments:  Report generator is very powerful and flexible.
    It can produce a variety of printed lists as user specifies.
```

SCORE: +++
          0   1   2   3   4   5

SECURITY:

```
    Passwords: user specified, at the field level_____
    Security from alteration: yes, read-only passwords_____
    Dial-up access: none_____
    Log on procedure: simple_____
    Usage tracking: saves all searches unless tell otherwise
    Back-up procedures: format creates batch input file copy
    Comments: Some problem with files getting corrupted for
    unknown reasons.  InMagic says they are working on fixing it.
```

SCORE: +++
          0   1   2   3   4   5

TRAINING/DOCUMENTATION:

```
    Amount of training needed: moderate_____
    Online tutorials: good_____
    Different user levels: no_____
    Printed tutorials: no_____
    Training by vendor: may do it for a fee_____
    Documentation: good_____
         Clarity: good_____
         Comprehensiveness: good_____
         Accuracy: seems to be accurate_____
    Other support materials: BiblioGuide formats for libraries
    Comments: Newsletter, user groups_____
    _____
```

SCORE: +++
          0   1   2   3   4   5

```
VENDOR OR PRODUCER:

     Knowledge of textual databases: extensive
     Other products: no other software, do consulting
     Years in business: over 10
     Reputation: good
     Date this product introduced: MS-DOS 1984
     Users of this product: variety of libraries and others
     (ask InMagic Inc. for an updated list)
     Users' reactions: generally positive
     Vendor accessibility: charge for phone support, toll call
     Support services: available for a fee
     Your reactions: generally positive
     Comments: user group plus some users locally.  Phone support
     fee may be a problem.

SCORE:    ++++++++++++++++++++++++++++++++++++++++++++++++++++++++++
          0          1          2          3          4          5


OTHER CONSIDERATIONS:

     Cost: $975.
     Cost compared with similar programs: ok
     Maintenance availability: None, except phone contract.
     Upgrade procedures: Users are notified of upgrades
     Lease/use restrictions: normal
     Comments: Communications package and word processing
     package will be needed for downloading and editing for batch.

SCORE:    ++++++++++++++++++++++++++++++++++++++++++++++++++++++++++
          0          1          2          3          4          5

**************************************************************

SUMMARY SCORE:     _____

FINAL COMMENTS: Report writer is very powerful and there are
library applications given in the BiblioGuide.  Searching gets
cumbersome for novice users.
```

SOFTWARE EVALUATION FORM

Name of package: Sci-Mate_____Version: 2.0_____
Producer: Institute for Scientific Information_____
Contact Person:_____Phone Number:800-523-4092
Address: 3501 Market Street, Philadelphia, PA 19104_____

****

GENERAL CONSIDERATIONS:

    Number of records supported: 32,767, but problems over 5000
    Number of fields per record: 20_____
    Restrictions on field lengths: effectively none, links records
    Variable length fields: yes_____
    Multiple Values per field: yes_____
    File Structures: signature files, inverted optional_
    Overhead: low for signature files, medium for inverted_
    User designated Index fields: yes_____
    DBMS or file manager: file manager_____
    Multiple user system: no_____
    Comments: Sci-Mate works best for files under 4 megabytes.
    Signature file structure means dynamic updates, low overhead.
    Sci-Mate is a three module package--Searcher, Manager and Editor)
SCORE: ++
          0   1   2   3   4   5
    (UNACCEPTABLE)   (POOR)   (FAIR)   (AVERAGE)   (GOOD)   (EXCELLENT)

HARDWARE REQUIREMENTS:

    Turnkey system: no_____
    Brand/model required: IBM PC and others_____
    Operating system(s): MS-DOS and CP/M_____
    Memory required: 256K for IBM, 64K for CP/M_____
    Peripherals required: none_____
    Other peripherals supported: modem with Searcher, hard disk
    Dedicated hardware required: no_____
    Comments:_____
    _____

SCORE: ++
          0   1   2   3   4   5

DATA INPUT:

```
    Variety of input means: Keyboard or batch, downloading ok
    Ease of input procedures: keyboard easy, batch moderate
    New input identified: yes, date stamps records at input
    User defined templates: yes
        Single or multiple templates per file: single
    Editing features: easy
        Screen editor or line editor: screen
        Global changes: no, must dump to word processor
        Ease of edit commands: easy
    Updating (batch or dynamic): both
    Data verification: none
    Look-up tables: none
    Comments: If the Searcher is used to download records, it
    is easy to transfer them to the Manager in batch.
```

SCORE: ++
           0   1   2   3   4   5

SEARCHING:

```
    Query language included: yes
    Menu driven or command: menu
    Ease of learning: very easy
    Error messages: ok, help sometimes available, menu choices
    Set building: no
    Boolean operators: AND, OR, AND NOT, nesting only if inverted
    Proximity searching: no
    Comparison or arithmetic operators: no
    Truncation: right and left hand
    Free text searching: yes
    All fields searchable: yes
    Individual fields searchable: yes
    Save and rerun searches: no
    Vocabulary control: no
    Comments: Quicksearch works on inverted fields. It allows
    nested parentheses but only right truncation. It is faster.
```

SCORE: ++
           0   1   2   3   4   5

OUTPUT:

```
Online screen display: Menus
Report generator: Separate package, Editor, for flexibility
     User defined formats: In Editor
     System supplied formats: yes, many bibliographic
     Ease of use: Editor is complex, Manager easy but limited
Sorting: single field
     User defined: yes
     System supplied: simple ones
     Entire database or subset: both
Arithmetic functions: none
Comments: Very simple columnar reports can be easily done
with the Manager module. For more or bibliographies, Editor needed.
```

```
SCORE:  ++++++++++++++++++++++++++++++++++++++++++++++++++++
        0         1         2         3         4         5
```

SECURITY:

```
Passwords: No
Security from alteration: None, delete is a menu option.
Dial-up access: no
Log on procedure: simple
Usage tracking: no
Back-up procedures: none
Comments: Security from alteration is one of the poorest
features of this package.
```

```
SCORE:  ++++++++++++++++++++++++++++++++++++++++++++++++++++
        0         1         2         3         4         5
```

TRAINING/DOCUMENTATION:

```
Amount of training needed: Little
Online tutorials: brief
Different user levels: no
Printed tutorials: no
Training by vendor: no
Documentation: good
     Clarity: very good
     Comprehensiveness: good
     Accuracy: seems good
Other support materials: newsletter for a fee
Comments: Phone support is available for a yearly fee.
System is so easy to use little training needed.
```

```
SCORE:  ++++++++++++++++++++++++++++++++++++++++++++++++++++
        0         1         2         3         4         5
```

VENDOR OR PRODUCER:

```
Knowledge of textual databases: Excellent
Other products: Commercial databases
Years in business: over 20
Reputation: excellent
Date this product introduced: 1983
Users of this product: researchers, libraries, see ISI
for current users.
Users' reactions:  generally positive
Vendor accessibility: 800 number.  Phone support for a fee.
Support services: see above
Your reactions: positive
Comments:
```

```
SCORE:   +++++++++++++++++++++++++++++++++++++++++++++++++++++++
         0         1         2         3         4         5
```

OTHER CONSIDERATIONS:

```
Cost: Each module is $395 or all 3 for $995.
Cost compared with similar programs: ok
Maintenance availability: none, except fee phone service
Upgrade procedures: users notified of upgrades
Lease/use restrictions: usual
Comments: Purchase of all three modules is desirable for
this application.
```

```
SCORE:   +++++++++++++++++++++++++++++++++++++++++++++++++++++++
         0         1         2         3         4         5
```

```
*****************************************************************
```

SUMMARY SCORE:

FINAL COMMENTS: The three modules work well together. Only
the Editor seems difficult to learn. The Manager is very user
friendly and easy. The Searcher will allow records to be downloaded and easily transferred to the Manager. Simple listings
with truncated titles can be generated by the Manager, but they
wouldn't be satisfactory in most cases.

BUILDING THE DATABASE

Here are two screen displays from Sci-Mate that show how the database was created. The first is a template that includes field names, whether or not the field is to have inverted indexes, and a two-letter code for the field. None of the fields in this database were indexed because the database is small. Larger databases (over several thousand records) should have inverted indexes for frequently searched fields.

Sci-Mate allows multiple templates for different types of documents and comes with some ready-made templates. Set-up time for this database is five minutes.

```
DISPLAY TEMPLATE 13           Name:  ONCOLOGY                    Source: bc
----------------------------------------------------------------------------

Field#  Name      Index  Code        Field#  Name      Index  Code
------  ----      -----  ----        ------  ----      -----  ----
   1    LOCATION    N     LO           11
   2    TITLE       N     TI           12
   3    AUTHOR      N     AU           13
   4    JOURNAL     N     JO           14
   5    CITATION    N     CI           15
   6    YEAR        N     YR           16
   7    SUBJECT     N     SU           17
   8    ABSTRACT    N     AB           18
   9                                   19
  10                                   20

DISPLAY Another Template?  (Y/N)
```

The following sample record is from Sci-Mate. The abstract is so long that two screens were required. Menu options always appear at the top of each screen:

```
DISPLAY AN 116              N=Next    E=Edit    L=Delete Hit/List S=Stop
Date 10/5/87               B=Back    P=Print   D=Delete/File
Source: BC    Template: 13   ENTER COMMAND:
```

```
LOCATION 87-0174
TITLE     Immunologic Classification of Childhood Acute Lymphcytic Leukemia.
AUTHOR    Foon, KA; Herzog, P; Billing, RJ: Terasake, PI: Feig, SA
JOURNAL   Cancer
CITATION  v. 47, n. 2, pp. 280-284, January 15
YEAR      1981
SUBJECT   Diagnosis; Surface membrane markers; Acute lumphocytic leukemia
ABSTRACT  Immunologic approaches to the classification of acute lymphocytic
          leukemia (ALL) have led to a new awareness of the heterogeneity of
          this disease.  Surface membrane markers including surface membrane
          immunoglobulin, complement receptors, and sheep erythrocyte (E)
          receptors have demonstrated at least three subtypes of ALL, which
          include non-B, non-T, ALL, T-ALL, and B-ALL.  In addition,
          hetero-antisera to Ia-like antigens and ALL-asociated antigens have
          been used to positively identify non-B, non-T ALL, which was
          previously a diagnosis of exclusion.  This paper reports 17 cases of
          childhood ALL whose lymphoblasts were studied for surface membrane
          immunoglobulin, sheep erythrocyte receptors, and the presence of
          four antigens detected by well-characterized heteroantisera.  Every
                                                    <^N> Next Page
```

Appendix B
Selected Software Packages

DBMS

DBase III Plus
Ashton-Tate
10150 W. Jefferson Blvd.
Culver City, CA 90230
(213) 204-5570

Helix, Double Helix
Odesta Corp.
4084 Commercial Ave.
Northbrook, IL 60062
(312) 498-5615

Knowledgeman 2
Micro Data Base Systems, Inc.
Box 248
Lafayette, IN 47902
(317) 436-2581

Paradox
Ansa Software
1301 Shoreway Rd.
Belmont, CA 94002
(415) 595-4469

R:BASE System V
Microrim Inc.
3380 146 Place S.E.
Bellevue, WA 98007
(206) 641-6619

Revelation, Advanced Revelation
Cosmos, Inc.
1346 14 Ave.
Box 1237

Longview, WA 98632
(206) 423-0763

Sequitur
Golemics, Inc.
2600 10 St.
Berkeley, CA 94710
(415)486-8347

FILE MANAGERS

askSam
Seaside Software
Box 31
Perry, FL 32347
(800) 3-ASKSAM

DayFlo TRACKER
Dayflo Software
17701 Mitchell Ave. N.
Irvine, CA 92714
(714) 474-1364

File
Microsoft Corp.
16011 N.E. 36 Way
Box 97017
Redmond, WA 98703
(206) 882-8080

Filemaker, Filemaker Plus
Forethought
250 Sobrante Way
Sunnyvale, CA 94086
(408) 737-7070

199

Nutshell, Nutshell Plus
Canterbury Intrntl.
Ashland Technology Centre
200 Homer Ave.
Ashland, MA 01721
(617) 881-7404

Q&A
Symantec Corp.
10201 Torre Ave.
Cupertino, CA 95014
(408) 253-9600

PC-File III, PC-File/R
Buttonware, Inc.
Box 5786
Bellevue, WA 98006
(206) 454-0479

PFS First Choice
PFS Professional File
Software Publishing Corp.
1901 Landings Dr.
Mountain View, CA 94043
(415) 962-8910

Savvy
The Savvy Corp.
122 Tulane S.E.
Albuquerque, NM 87106
(505) 265-1273

FYI3000
FYI, Inc.
4202 Spicewood Rd. #204
Box 26481
Austin, TX 78755
(512) 346-0133

TEXT RETRIEVAL PACKAGES

BlueFish
Computer Access Corp.
26 Brighton St.
Belmont, MA 02178-4008

Dragnet
Access Softek
3204 Adeline St.
Berkeley, CA 94703
(415) 654-0116

Electra Find, Text Collector
O'Neill Software
Box 26111
San Francisco, CA 94126
(415) 398-2255

Ful/Text
Fulcrum Technologies
560 Rochester St.
Ottawa, Ontario, Canada
(613) 238-1761

Gofer
Microlytics, Inc.
300 Main St.
East Rochester, NY 14445
(800) 828-6293, (716) 248-9150

Memory Lane, TEXTBANK
Group L Corp.
481 Carlisle Dr.
Herndon, VA 22070
(703) 471-0030

SearchExpress
Executive Technologies, Inc.
2120 Sixteenth Ave. S.
Birmingham, AL 35205
(205) 933-5494

ZyINDEX
Zylab Corporation
233 E. Erie St.
Chicago, IL 60611
(312) 642-2201

411
Select Information Systems, Inc.
919 Sir Francis Drake Blvd.
Kentfield, CA 94904

INFORMATION STORAGE AND RETRIEVAL PACKAGES

BRS/Search for Micros
BRS Software Group
1200 Rte. 7
Latham, NY 12100
(800) 833-4707

CAIRS
Information/Documentation, Inc.
Box 17109, Dulles International
 Airport
Washington, DC 20041
(800) 336-0800

CAIRS Marketing and Support
Leatherhead Food Research
 Association
Randalls Road
Leatherhead, Surrey, KT22 7RY
England
(0372) 376761

Concept Finder
MMIMS, Inc.
566A S. York Rd.
Elmhurst, IL 60126
(312) 941-0090

Finder
Finder Information Tools, Inc.
1430 W. Peachtree St.
Atlanta, GA 30309
(404) 872-3488

INMAGIC
InMagic Inc.
238 Broadway
Cambridge, MA 02139
(617) 661-8124

Marcon II
AIRS, Inc.
Engineering Research Center
335 Paint Branch Dr.

College Park, MD 20742
(301) 454-2022

Pro-Cite
(also Biblio-Links and Pro-Search)
Personal Bibliographic Software,
 Inc.
412 Longshore
Ann Arbor, MI 48105
(313) 996-1580

Sci-Mate Software System
(File Manager, Editor and Searcher)
Institute for Scientific Information

Sci-Mate Customer Services
3501 Market St.
Philadelphia, PA 19104
(800) 523-4092

Personal Librarian (formerly) SIRE
Cucumber Information Systems
5611 Kraft Dr.
Rockville, MD 20852
(301) 984-3539

STAR
Cuadra Associates, Inc.
2001 Wilshire Blvd.
Santa Monica, CA 90403
(213) 829-9972

LIBRARY APPLICATIONS

Advance
Advanced Library Concepts
Box 62029
Honolulu, HI 96839
(808) 942-9773

Card Datalog
Data Trek, Inc.
121 West E St.
Encinitas, CA 92024
(619) 436-5055

M/Series 10
(formerly InfoQUEST)
UTLAS Intrntl.
1611 North Kent St.
Arlington, VA 22209
(703) 525-5940

Mandarin
Media Flex Inc.
Box 1107
Champlain, NY 12919
(518) 298-2970

Micro Library System
Sydney Dataproducts, Inc.
11075 Santa Monica Blvd.
Los Angeles, CA 90025
(213) 479-4621

Ocelot
ABALL Software Inc.
2174 Hamilton St.
Regina, Saskatchewan,
 Canada
S4P 2E6
(306) 569-2180

TINman
Information Management and
 Engineering Ltd.
14-16 Farringdon Lane
London EC1M 3AU
England
44(0)1 253 1177

BIBLIOGRAPHY GENERATORS

Notebook II with Bibliography
Pro/Tem Software, Inc.
2363 Boulevard Circle
Walnut Creek, CA 94595
(800) 826-2222

Pro-Cite
see under Information Storage and
 Retrieval

Sci-Mate Editor
see under Information Storage and
 Retrieval

Reference Manager
Research Information Systems Inc.
1991 Village Park Way
Encinitas, CA 92024
(619) 753-3914

Appendix C
Selected Software Directories

Auerbach Software Reports
Auerbach Publishers Inc.
6560 N. Park Dr.
Pennsauken, NJ 08109
Updated monthly, looseleaf.

A Buyer's Guide to Data Base Management Systems
Datapro Research Corporation
1805 Underwood Blvd.
Delran, NJ 08075
Updated annually. Selected from Datapro 70.

Datapro 70
Datapro Research Corporation
1805 Underwood Blvd.
Delran, NJ 08075
Updated monthly, looseleaf.

Datapro Directory of Microcomputer Software
Datapro Research Corporation
1805 Underwood Blvd.
Delran, NJ 08075
Updated monthly, looseleaf.

Directory of Automated Library Systems
Joseph R. Matthews
Neal-Schuman Publishers, Inc.
23 Leonard St.
New York, NY 10013

Directory of Computer Software Applications: Library and Information Sciences

National Technical Information
Service
5285 Port Royal Rd.
Springfield, VA 22161
(1978-September 1980).

Directory of Information Management Software: For Libraries, Information Centers, Record Centers, 1987/88 edition
Edited by Edward Kazlauskas and Pamela Cibbarelli
Pacific Information Inc.
11684 Ventura Blvd.
Studio City, CA 91604
Distributed by the American Library Association
50 E. Huron St.
Chicago, IL 60611

A Directory of Library and Information Retrieval Software for Microcomputers, 2nd edition
Compiled by Hilary Dyer and Alison Brookes
Gower Publishing Company Ltd.
Gower House
Croft Rd.
Farnborough
Hants GV14 7RU
England

Gower Publishing Company
Old Post Rd.
Brookfield, VT 05036

*Directory of Microcomputer Software
  for Libraries*
Edited by Robert A. Walton and
  Nancy Taylor
Oryx Press
2214 N. Central
Phoenix, AZ 85004

*The Library Microconsumer: MRC's
  Guide to Library Software*
Edited by Robert M. Mason
Metrics Research Corporation
11000 Cedar Ave. 4th fl.
Cleveland, OH 44106

Micro Software Report: Library Edition
Edited by Jeanne Nolan
Meckler Publishing Company
11 Ferry Lane West
Westport, CT 06880

Microcomputers for Libraries
Edited by James E. Rush
James E. Rush Associates, Inc.
2223 Carriage Rd.
Powell, OH 43065

MicroUse Directory: Software
Edited by Ching-chih Chen
MicroUse Information
1400 Commonwealth Ave.
West Newton, MA 02165

Mini-Micro Software
A.P. Publications Ltd.
322 St. John St.
London, EC1V 4QH
England
Quarterly.

*OMNI Complete Catalog of Comput-
  er Software*
Collier Books, Macmillan Publishing
  Company
866 Third Ave.
New York, NY 10022

*101 Software Packages to Use in Your
  Library: Descriptions, Evaluations,
  Practical Advice*
Patrick Dewey
American Library Association
50 E. Huron St.
Chicago, IL 60611

*Online Micro Software Guide and
  Directory*
Online Inc.
11 Tannery Lane
Westport, CT 06883

PC Tech Journal
Volume 5, no. 13, 1988, pp. 425–488

*Text Retrieval: A Directory of
  Software, 2nd edition*
Edited by Robert Kimberley
Gower Publishing Company Ltd.
Gower House
Croft Rd.
Farnborough
Hants GV14 7RU
England

*The Software Catalog—
  Microcomputers*
Elsevier Science Publishing Co.,
  Inc.
Box 1663
Grand Central Station
New York, NY 10163-1663

*UNESCO Inventory of Software
  Packages*
National Center of Scientific and
  Technological Information
Box 20215
Tel-Aviv, Israel

Whole Earth Software Catalog
Quantum Press/Doubleday
501 Franklin Ave.
Garden City, NY 11530

ONLINE DIRECTORIES

Business Software Database
File 256 on DIALOG
Information Sources, Inc., Berkeley,
Calif.

MENU—The International Software
Database
File 232 on DIALOG
International Software Database
Corp., Fort Collins, Colo.

Microcomputer Software and Hardware Guide

File 278 on DIALOG
R.R. Bowker Company, New York,
N.Y.

Online Microcomputer Software
Guide and Directory
File SOFT on BRS
Online Inc., Weston, Conn.

ON FLOPPY DISK

PC-DBDB
Shadduck and Sullivan
Information Specialists
3508 45th Ave. S.
Minneapolis, MN 55406

Appendix D
Selected Sources of Software Reviews

LIBRARY ORIENTED SOURCES

Database
Online, Inc.
11 Tannery Lane
Weston, CT 06883

The Electronic Library
Learned Information, Inc.
143 Old Marlton Pike
Medford, NJ 08055

Library Hi Tech
Pierian Press
Box 1808
Ann Arbor, MI 48106

Library Software Review
Meckler Publishing Corporation
11 Ferry Lane West
Westport, CT 06880

Micro Software Evaluations
Meckler Publishing Corporation
11 Ferry Lane West
Westport, CT 06880

*Microcomputers for Information
  Management*
Ablex Publishing Corp.
355 Chestnut St.
Norwood, NJ 07648

Online
Online, Inc.
11 Tannery Lane
Weston, CT 06883

Online Review
Learned Information, Inc.
143 Old Marlton Pike
Medford, NJ 08055

Small Computers in Libraries
Meckler Publishing Corporation
11 Ferry Lane West
Westport, CT 06880

GENERAL MICROCOMPUTER
SOURCES

Byte
McGraw Hill, Inc.
One Phoenix Mill Lane
Peterborough, NH 03458

InfoWorld
1060 Marsh Rd.
Menlo Park, CA 94025

PC Magazine
Ziff-Davis Publishing Company
One Park Ave.
New York, NY 10016

PC World
PCW Communications, Inc.
501 Second St.
San Francisco, CA 94107

Whole Earth Software Review
Box 27956
San Diego, CA 92128

ONLINE SOURCES

Computer Database
File 275 on DIALOG
Information Access Company, Belmont, Calif.

ERIC
File 1 on DIALOG, File ERIC on BRS
Also available from many other systems
National Institute of Education, Washington, D.C.
ERIC Processing and Reference Facility, Bethesda, Md.

Information Science Abstracts
File 202 on DIALOG
IFI/Plenum Data Company, Alexandria, Va.

INSPEC
File 13 on DIALOG, File INSP on BRS
The Institution of Electrical Engineers, London, England

Library and Information Science Abstracts (LISA)
File 61 on DIALOG
Library Association Publishing, London, England

Magazine Index
File 47 on DIALOG, File MAGS on BRS

Information Access Company, Belmont, Calif.

Microcomputer Index
File 233 on DIALOG
Database Services, Los Altos, Calif.

Reader's Guide to Periodical Literature
File RDG on WILSONLINE
H.W. Wilson Company, Bronx, N.Y.

CONFERENCE PROCEEDINGS

American Society for Information Science
Learned Information Inc.
143 Old Marlton Pike
Medford, NJ 08055

International Online Meeting
Learned Information Ltd.
Besselsleigh Road
Abingdon, Oxford OX13 6LG
England

National Online Meeting
Learned Information Inc.
143 Old Marlton Pike
Medford, NJ 08055

Online Conference
Online, Inc.
11 Tannery Lane
Westport, CT 06883

Glossary

ABSTRACT: An accurate and concise summary of the contents of a document. A value-added field that is added to a record to enhance retrieval and aid relevance judgment.

ACCESS POINT: A part of a record that can be specified in a search.

APPLICATIONS SOFTWARE: Computer programs written to accomplish some specific user-oriented task, such as word processing or library circulation control.

ASCII: American Standard Code for Information Interchange. A standard code for representing computer-readable characters using seven bits.

AUTHORITY FILE: A file or list of standardized, verified entries (such as authors names, subjects, companies, and so on) with cross-references from unacceptable forms to used forms.

BACKUP: To provide added file copies or hardware in order to recover from loss or hardware failure.

BAUD: Speed of data transmission in signal elements per second. At low speeds signal elements are single bits; at higher speeds signal elements generally contain more than one bit. For high speed transmission, bits per second (BPS) is preferred.

BIBLIOGRAPHIC DATABASE: A file that contains surrogate records describing and pointing to documents.

BIBLIOGRAPHIC UTILITY: An organization that provides access to bibliographic databases primarily for library cataloging and related activities.

BIBLIOGRAPHY GENERATOR: Special purpose software that produces correctly formatted bibliographies from bibliographic records.

BIT (BINARY DIGIT): The smallest unit of information in a computer. A bit is either a one or a zero. A combination of bits in a byte represents a character.

BOOLEAN OPERATORS: Typically AND, OR and NOT, Boolean operators allow logical combinations of search words or phrases.

AND narrows a search by requiring both terms to be in one document, OR broadens a search by allowing either term to be present, and NOT excludes documents.

BYTE: A group of bits which represents a character or symbol within the character set of the computer. There are usually eight bits to a byte.

CD-ROM (Compact Disk-Read Only Memory): A 4.75-inch optical digital disk. The disk is mastered, and users can neither write to the disk nor erase information.

CHARACTER: A letter, numeric digit, punctuation, or other special symbol used to record information.

CHARACTER SET: The set of characters that can be dealt with by a particular piece of equipment. ASCII is a standard code for representing a character set.

COMPARISON OPERATORS: Typically greater than, less than, equal to, greater than or equal to, less than or equal to, and not equal to. Used to search for terms or numbers in these relationships.

CONTROLLED VOCABULARY: Either a term authority file or thesaurus; a controlled vocabulary is used when adding subject descriptors to a database to ensure consistent use of word forms.

CPU (Central Processing Unit): The part of a computer that performs the data manipulation.

DATA: Recorded observations, values to be processed by the computer.

DATABASE MANAGEMENT SYSTEMS (DBMS): Special purpose software designed to process information in groups of related files.

DATABASE: Any collection of information in machine-readable form made searchable on a computer. May be bibliographic, referral, full text, or numeric.

DATA DICTIONARY: A file for machine and/or human consumption that lists and defines data elements including name, format, and meaning.

Directory Database. See **REFERRAL DATABASE.**

DOCUMENTATION: The manuals that tell users, maintainers, and database designers about the software.

DOUBLE POSTED: Fields that are both phrase and word parsed in the inverted indexes.

DOWNLOAD: To transfer information from a larger computer (such as an online vendor's system) to a smaller computer (such as the searcher's microcomputer.)

FEEDBACK: Response to system action, used to alter the behavior of the system.

FIELDS: Records in a database are typically broken into units to store related data such as titles or authors.

FILE: A collection of records or machine-readable information.

FILE MANAGER: Software designed to perform additions, deletion, searching, and other functions for a single file of information.

FULL-TEXT DATABASE: The complete texts of journal articles, books, newspapers, or the like available in machine-readable form. Full-text databases do not as yet include graphics.

HASHING: The translation of a primary access point (key) into a disk address by applying a mathematical formula.

HIERARCHICAL DATA MODEL: Organization of data records based on relationships that follow a tree structure or hierarchy.

HARDWARE: The physical components of a computer system.

HIT: A record that satisfies a query in an information retrieval system.

INFORMATION STORAGE AND RETRIEVAL SYSTEM (IS&R): In general, a system that supports the input, storage, updating, and retrieval of information. More narrowly used in this book to refer to such a system applied to structured textual information, such as bibliographic records. IS&R systems typically have powerful and flexible retrieval capabilities.

INHOUSE DATABASE: A collection of computer searchable information created by an organization or an individual for use within that organization or by that individual.

INTEGRATED CIRCUIT: A complex electronic component consisting of many transistors manufactured on a single chip of (usually) silicon.

INTERFACE: The connection between two systems, two parts of a system, or the user and the system.

INVERTED INDEX FILE: A file that consists of words or phrases taken from the linear file of a database. Inverted indexes facilitate fast searching.

KEYWORD: A word from a record that may be used for retrieval.

LINEAR FILE: A file containing the primary records in a database, usually in accession number order.

LOCAL AREA NETWORK (LAN): A network used to link computers and other computer resources within a local area such as an office, a building, or a group of buildings.

Machine indexing. See **INVERTED INDEX FILE** and **PARSING.**

MACHINE-READABLE FORM: Data encoded and recorded on a medium which will allow input into a computer system.

MARC FORMAT: Machine-readable cataloging, a standard

way to code and describe bibliographic information in machine-readable form. Used by libraries.

MEGABYTE: One million bytes.

MENU: A list of options presented on a video display terminal so that the user can make a selection.

MICROCOMPUTER: A small, relatively inexpensive computer, based on a microprocessor form of CPU.

MICROPROCESSOR: A single chip containing a CPU.

MODEM: A device that converts digital signals to analog for transmission over telephone lines or other analog media, and from analog to digital when receiving.

NUMERIC DATABASE: A collection of statistical information or other numbers made searchable on a computer.

OPAC: Online Public Access Catalog.

ONLINE: The mode of computer use where the user is seeking information from the computer while the computer is processing, usually interactive. Often used to refer to remote online; the user is connected to a host vendor via a modem.

ONLINE VENDOR: An organization that has computers, storage devices, and software to make databases available for remote access online searching.

OPTICAL CHARACTER RECOGNITION (OCR): Data conversion technique in which a device recognizes typed characters and converts them to machine-readable form.

OPERATING SYSTEM: A program that manages the operation and resources of a computer.

OPTICAL DIGITAL DISK: Storage medium; data in the form of ones and zeros are directly written by laser.

PACKET SWITCHING: The transmission of data in small blocks (or packets) with destination and sequence information included in each packet. The packets are routed through the communication network from node-to-node via the best available route, which may not be the same for all packets in a message. Packets are reassembled at their destination.

PARITY: A method of checking for errors in data transmission whereby an additional bit is added to each byte to make the number of ones even (even parity) or odd (odd parity).

PARSING: The process of machine indexing, in which the computer software pulls words or phrases from the linear file of records to be put into an inverted index for searching.

PERIPHERAL: Any of several devices attached to a computer to support its operation (e.g., printer, disk drive, or light pen).

PHRASE PARSING: The extraction of multiword entries into an inverted index. Special delimiters are used to indicate the end of an entry.

POSTCOORDINATED: The process by which the software puts related words together at output. Implies the ability to do Boolean combinations or proximity searching.

PRECOORDINATED: Multiword terms that are linked together at the time of input.

PROGRAM: A sequence of instructions written in a special language, which when translated into machine code and executed will perform a desired task.

PROXIMITY OPERATORS: A search feature that allows words in a record to be searched in a specified relationship, e.g., adjacent to each other, within a specified number of words, in the same sentence, or in the same paragraph.

RAM (RANDOM ACCESS MEMORY): The internal memory in a computer that is used to store instructions and data during the running of a program.

RANGE SEARCHING: The process of specifying a range of values, such as from 1980 to 1985, for searching.

RECORD: Information about a particular item in a file. Often subdivided into fields.

REFERRAL DATABASE: A database that contains directory information such as names, addresses, and other information about people, companies, software, and so on.

SEQUENTIAL SEARCHING: The mode of searching in which every record is examined in turn to determine if it satisfies retrieval criteria.

SOFTWARE: Computer programs, instructions which the computer needs to operate.

STOP WORDS: Trivial or noninformative words that are not included in the inverted index. Either database designer defined or software defined.

STRING SEARCHING: Searching process in which a sequence of characters in a query is matched on a character-by-character basis with a sequence of characters in the record.

SUBJECT DESCRIPTORS: Words added to records to describe the contents of an item. Value-added.

SUPERIMPOSED HASHING: A coding technique that produces a fixed length string of bits in a pattern that is derived from a mathematical transformation (hashing) of the character sequence in a record. Used in place of an inverted index for rapid retrieval.

SYSTEM SOFTWARE: Computer programs that perform tasks associated with the general operation of the computer. (See also OPERATING SYSTEM.)

TEXT RETRIEVAL SOFTWARE: A computer-based system for storage and searching of unstructured text.

THESAURUS: A list of the terms in a controlled vocabulary, usually including accepted terms with cross references from unaccepted terms and hierarchical relationships between terms.

TRUNCATION: The capability of searching for all words that contain the same specified word stem.

TURNKEY SYSTEM: A computer system sold for a particular application in which both software and hardware are included as an integrated package.

VALIDATION: The checking of data that are input to ensure their accuracy. Usually refers to a computer performing this checking.

VALUE-ADDED FIELDS: Any field added to a record that enhances the record. Usually added by intellectual processing, such as subject descriptor indexing or abstracting.

WORD-ORIENTED DATABASES: Databases that contain mostly words or text rather than numbers. Can be bibliographic, full-text, or referral.

WORD PARSING: The extraction of single words to be placed into an inverted index for searching.

WORM (WRITE ONCE READ MANY): An optical digital medium that allows a user to write to the disk but not erase.

Subject Index

Author Index